"Like Sheep at the Slaughter"

A Statistical History of the Fourth Rhode Island Volunteers

Robert Grandchamp

HERITAGE BOOKS
2018

HERITAGE BOOKS
AN IMPRINT OF HERITAGE BOOKS, INC.

Books, CDs, and more—Worldwide

For our listing of thousands of titles see our website
at
www.HeritageBooks.com

Published 2018 by
HERITAGE BOOKS, INC.
Publishing Division
5810 Ruatan Street
Berwyn Heights, Md. 20740

Copyright © 2018 Robert Grandchamp

Heritage Books by the author:

From Providence to Fort Hell: Letters from Company K, Seventh Rhode Island Volunteers

"In Te Domine Speramus": Essays on Rhode Island Military History

"Like Sheep at the Slaughter": A Statistical History of the Fourth Rhode Island Volunteers

"Now Show Them What Rhode Island Can Do!": An Annotated Bibliography of Rhode Island Civil War Sources

"We Lost Many Brave Men": A Statistical History of the Seventh Rhode Island Volunteers

"With their usual ardor": Scituate, Rhode Island and the American Revolution

All rights reserved. No part of this book may be reproduced or transmitted in any form or by any means, electronic or mechanical, including photocopying, recording or by any information storage and retrieval system without written permission from the author, except for the inclusion of brief quotations in a review.

International Standard Book Number
Paperbound: 978-0-7884-5851-4

"Our men fell like sheep at the slaughter"

-Corporal George H. Allen

Company B, Fourth Rhode Island Volunteers

September 17, 1862

For Addison Hope

CONTENTS

A brief history of the Fourth Rhode Island	1
Methodology	9
Field and Staff	15
Regimental Band	21
Company A	23
Company B	37
Company C	53
Company D	69
Company E	83
Company F	97
Company G	109
Company H	123
Company I	137
Company K	151
Enlistments by town	163
Regimental Statistics	165
The Rhode Island Dead at Newbern	179

Further Reading	183
Acknowledgments	189
About the Author	193

A BRIEF HISTORY OF THE FOURTH RHODE ISLAND

Known as the "Fighting Fourth," the Fourth Rhode Island Volunteers was the last infantry unit raised in Rhode Island in 1861. After Union setbacks in the West, and after the humiliating defeat at Bull Run, the regiment had no trouble recruiting ten companies from throughout the state in August and September 1861. The men of the Fourth were true volunteers who enlisted before large bounties became an enticement to enlist. Among those who enlisted was Calixa Lavallee, a Quebecois emigrant who joined as a musician in the regimental band. After the war, Lavallee returned to Quebec and wrote the lyrics to "O Canada!," which eventually became the Canadian National Anthem.

The companies of the regiment were recruited as follows:

Company A: Providence

Company B: Providence

Company C: Providence

Company D: Burrillville, Glocester, and Hopkinton

Company E: Smithfield and Woonsocket

Company F: Providence

Company G: Middletown and Newport

Company H: North Kingstown

Company I: Pawtucket

Company K: Warwick

In addition, the American Brass Band of Providence, which had formerly volunteered for service with the First Rhode Island Detached Militia volunteered again as the regimental band. After regimental bands were forbidden in the summer of 1862, the bandsmen were mustered out shortly after Antietam.

The regiment was originally commanded by Colonel Justus I. McCarthy, a tough Old Army Regular who only held the command for a few weeks before a falling out with Governor William Sprague led him to resign. He was replaced by Isaac Peace Rodman of South Kingstown. Although often written, Rodman was not a Quaker but rather a devout Baptist who owned, with his brother Rowland, a mill in Peace Dale. The war was starting to take a toll on the mills, as they began to suffer a lack of raw material, cotton, from the South; soon Rodman would sell the mill to the Hazard family. A member of the pre-war Narragansett Guards, Rodman raised Company E of the Second Rhode Island Volunteers and led the company at Bull Run, becoming the first Union infantry engaged in the fighting. Promotion followed that fall, and he became the colonel of the Fourth Rhode Island.

The Fourth Rhode Island, as was typical of most Rhode Island regiments had a well-trained and dedicated medical staff. Surgeon Henry W. Rivers was a well-respected Providence physician who would rise to medical director of the Ninth Corps. The Fourth lost fewer men to illness than any other Rhode Island regiment, a testament to the medical services provided by the staff. The Fourth was the only unit from Rhode Island where combat deaths outnumbered deaths to illness and accidents.

Originally sent to Washington, the Fourth soon joined Ambrose Burnside as part of his "Coast Division," which later formed the nucleus of the Ninth Corps. Sailing to the coast of North Carolina, the Fourth participated in the Battle of Roanoke

Island in February 1862. On March 14, the Fourth participated in its first pitched battle at New Bern. Advancing under heavy fire, Colonel Rodman saw a gap in the Confederate line and ordered a bayonet charge. Rodman's men surged forward, capturing several pieces of artillery, and the guidon of Latham's North Carolina Battery. In his after-action report, Burnside credited the Fourth as being the reason the Union troops won the battle. For his actions, Rodman became a brigadier general. Following the battle, the Fourth participated in the Siege of Fort Macon and later garrisoned New Bern.

In August 1862, the Fourth, now part of the Third Division of the Ninth Corps, moved to Newport News, Virginia. Here Governor Sprague appointed Lieutenant Colonel W.H.P. Steere of the Second Rhode Island to the vacant colonelcy of the regiment, sidestepping Lieutenant Colonel William Tew of the Fourth. When the news reached the regiment, half of the officers resigned on the spot, while the new colonel was physically assaulted by his men, as they mutinied, failing to respond to Steere's commands. A furious Sprague personally went to Newport News to settle the situation, commissioning new officers, and placing Captain Joseph B. Curtis as second in command of the regiment. With new officers, and new recruits following a recruiting drive in Rhode Island, the regiment slowly marched north into Maryland in pursuit of Lee's Army. On September 14, the Fourth was under fire during the Battle of South Mountain, losing several wounded.

On September 17, 1862, at Antietam, the Fourth took part in the horrendous fighting at Otto's Cornfield, a forty-acre entanglement on the southern edge of the battlefield. The Fourth went into action at Antietam with 247 officers and men. The regiment formed the extreme left flank of the Army of the Potomac. Unable to locate the enemy in the dense corn, several men were sent forward to reconnoiter, and the color bearer was killed. The Fourth Rhode Island engaged the foe, but the enemy, a brigade of South Carolinians, soon gained the exposed left flank of the regiment. Corporal George H. Allen recalled, "Our men fell like sheep at the slaughter." Colonel Steere was severely wounded early in the fighting, but gained the respect of his men for his leadership that day. Josiah and Jeremiah Moon were twin brothers from Coventry who marched side by side that day; Josiah was killed by the side of his twin.

Corporal Benjamin F. Burdick of Hopkinton died trying to save his boyhood friend Henry Freeman Saunders, who was also shot dead in the terrific blasts of musketry. The Sixteenth Connecticut was on the Fourth's right flank. They were a newly organized unit whose men had not even had time to learn how to load their muskets; the Sixteenth broke and ran, leaving the Fourth alone to face an entire Confederate brigade. General Rodman tried to rally the line, but was shot in the chest, and died two weeks later. He would be the highest ranking Rhode Islander to die in the Civil War. Finally, under immense pressure, the Fourth Rhode Island was routed, as the men ran for their lives, leaving half of the regiment, dead, wounded, or missing on the field. Twenty members of the regiment deserted in the face of the enemy that day and were never seen again. Many of the dead from the Fourth would later be laid to rest at Antietam National Cemetery.

Three months later, at Fredericksburg, the Fourth was again under fire, where Lieutenant Colonel Curtis became the regiment's only fatality, killed when an artillery shell burst overhead, and a piece struck him in the head. As the Fourth formed up to assault Marye's Heights, a lieutenant in Battery D, First Rhode Island Light Artillery reminded the men, "Boys, Remember that old Rhode Island is looking at you to-day." A witty private in Company B, watching the battle unfold to the front replied, "By jabbers, we'd rather be looking at Rhode Island about these times."

While the rest of the Ninth Corps was sent to Kentucky in February 1863, the Third Division, Ninth Corps, which included the Fourth was sent to Newport News, Virginia. The regiment spent most of 1863 and 1864, garrisoning a line of fortifications near Portsmouth, Virginia, occasionally coming under fire. They took part in a reconnaissance in force on the Confederate positions near Suffolk on May 3, 1863, losing several men. The winter of

1864 was spent at Point Lookout, Maryland, guarding Confederate prisoners of war. In mid-July 1864, the Fourth was ordered to rejoin the Army of the Potomac, then besieging the Army of Northern Virginia at Petersburg. The regiment was assigned to the First Brigade, Second Division, Ninth Corps, which also included the Seventh Rhode Island Volunteers.

The Fourth was under fire daily in the Petersburg entrenchments, losing men with each passing day. Having avoided the entirety of the Overland Campaign, the return to combat in the Petersburg trenches was a harrowing experience for the men. Three Myrick brothers from Coventry had volunteered in the fall of 1861 to serve in Company B of the Fourth. Private Samuel Myrick was killed at New Bern, while his older brother, Sergeant Cromwell P. Myrick died at Petersburg, leaving Solomon Myrick alone to return home.

On July 30, 1864, the Fourth advanced on the city in the fiasco that became known as the Battle of the Crater. Pinned down in "the horrid pit," a third of the regiment became casualties, with some men choosing capture instead of risking their lives to cross the pit to run away. When the United States flag went down, Private James Welsh of Smithfield grabbed the colors, and ran back to the Union line, earning the Medal of Honor. The Crater was the last major engagement for the Fourth, as they were now reduced to barely one hundred men present for duty. The regiment was largely held in reserve the rest of the summer, but took part in skirmishing at Weldon Railroad and Hatcher's Run.

On the morning of September 30, 1864 the Fourth was due to be pulled off the line to be sent back to Rhode Island to be mustered out. At the same time, however, the Ninth Corps was due to advance into battle once more at Poplar Spring Church. The Fourth volunteered to go into combat one last time. Advancing towards Poplar Spring Church, a shell exploded in the midst of the color guard, killing three men whose enlistments were nearly expired. The following day, the regiment was relieved, and returned to Providence to a hero's welcome.

While the majority of the regiment returned to Rhode Island, some 226 officers and men who had reenlisted or had enlisted after 1861 remained in the field. Consolidated into a three company battalion, these men were combined with the Seventh Rhode Island Volunteers, a unit that had also lost heavily in the 1864 battles. The consolidation with the Seventh did not sit too well with the veterans of the Fourth; they nearly mutinied again. They felt that they had earned the right to continue to be called the Fourth, the regiment they had enlisted in. Corporal George H. Allen recalled in his memoirs, "We were *once* and *always*, the Fourth Rhode Island Regiment." Lieutenant Colonel Percy Daniels of the Seventh Rhode Island was equally despised by the men of the Seventh, as well as the Fourth. Daniels assigned the men of the Fourth to the most hazardous part of Fort Hell, which the Seventh was garrisoning in front of Petersburg, Virginia, and demanded they perform constant picket and fatigue duty.

After a miserable winter at Fort Hell, the Seventh took part in the pursuit to Appomattox. Moving back to Washington, the veterans of the Fourth welcomed back a number of comrades who had been captured at the Crater and were now released from Confederate prisons. The consolidated regiment took part in the Grand Review of the Army of the Potomac. On June 9, 1865, the original members of the Seventh Rhode Island were mustered out and returned to Providence, leaving some 200 men of the original Fourth in the field, still under the name of the Seventh Rhode Island. Finally on July 13, 1865, the remaining veterans of the Fourth returned to Providence for mustering out. Unfortunately, a torrential rainstorm prevented a planned parade and reception.

After the war, the men of the Fourth, like the other Rhode Island regiments formed a veteran's association and met yearly on July 30, the anniversary of the Battle of the Crater. The bad blood between the veterans of the Fourth and the Seventh continued after the war as well, as men from neither regiment attended the other's reunions. As time went on, the Fourth Rhode Island became a forgotten regiment, overshadowed by the deeds performed by the Second and Seventh Rhode Island Volunteers, as well as the First Rhode Island Light Artillery. In 1887, Corporal George H. Allen published his wartime diary as *Forty-Six Months with the Fourth R.I. Volunteers, in the War of 1861 to 1865 Comprising a History of Its Marches, Battles, and Camp Life. Compiled from Journals Kept While on Duty in the Field and Camp, by Corp. Geo. H. Allen.* The book was adopted by the Fourth Rhode Island Veteran's Association as their official regimental history. A planned regimental monument at Antietam never occurred. Instead, the veterans of the Fourth joined veterans of the Fifth Rhode Island Heavy Artillery and Battery F, First Rhode Island Light Artillery in dedicating a monument to the Rhode Islanders who fell in the Burnside Expedition and elsewhere in North Carolina. The monument was erected in 1908 at the New Bern National Cemetery.

Private Elisha R. Watson was the last survivor of both the Fourth Rhode Island and the Seventh Rhode Island. A resident of Coventry, he enlisted in Company D of the Fourth in August 1862 and fought at Antietam and Fredericksburg. He lost his best friend to disease in February 1863. Watson was captured at the Crater and spent nine months as a prisoner of war. After his release from prison, Watson served in Company G of the Seventh Rhode Island Volunteers until his muster out. After the war he founded a postal shipping business, and raised a family. He was a very active member of McGregor Post #14 of the Grand Army of the Republic, and estimated that he visited nearly a thousand graves each Decoration Day; he was meticulous in his knowledge and carefully recorded each grave for postcrity. Watson was a frequent visitor to schools in the Pawtuxet Valley, reveling children about his wartime service. He died in April 1939 and was laid to rest at Knotty Oak Cemetery in Coventry.

Captain Sumner U. Shearman was one of many veterans of the Fourth Rhode Island Volunteers. A Brown University graduate, Shearman joined the regiment just in time to participate in the Maryland Campaign. He was captured at the Crater and endured nine months of captivity. After the war, he became a minister. In one of the best quotes written by a Rhode Island veteran, Shearman summed up his military service in the Fourth Rhode Island. "I have never regretted my being in the army during that most trying and critical period of our country. I feel as did the Westerner who said that he would not part with his experiences for a hundred thousand dollars, and he would not go through with it again for a hundred million."

For their services during the war, General Ulysses S. Grant ordered that the following battle honors be inscribed on the colors of the Fourth Rhode Island Volunteers: Roanoke Island, New Bern, Fort Macon, South Mountain, Antietam, Fredericksburg, Suffolk, Petersburg, Weldon Railroad, Hatcher's Run, and Poplar Spring Church.

The following history was extracted from George H. Allen's *Forty-Six Months with the Fourth R.I. Volunteers*, as well as the official records of the regiment at the Rhode Island State Archives.

METHODOLOGY

The following roster of the Fourth Rhode Island Volunteers was carefully transcribed from the original muster rolls and descriptive books held at the Rhode Island State Archives. The roster lists all the men known to have actually served in the regiment from 1861-1864, and does not include those who deserted before the regiment was mustered in on September 30, 1861. In certain cases additional information regarding casualties, deserters, and those who died at home has been added to the register from sources including Rhode Island newspapers, town hall records, the letters and journals of members of the Fourth Rhode Island, pension and service records, as well as the personal observations by this writer in the cemeteries of Rhode Island and elsewhere. Unlike many other regiments, the Fourth was very fortunate in that their regimental adjutant, Lieutenant Henry Joshua Spooner was a meticulous records keeper. His neat handwriting and methodical record keeping ability preserved the invaluable papers of the regiment for posterity.

Although some information might not be supported by what is listed in the "official records," this roster represents the most complete and accurate set of data of the officers and men who served in the Fourth Rhode Island Volunteers. Furthermore, when known, the date of death and burial location of the veteran has been identified. To identify burial locations, each soldier was run through three databases, namely www.findagrave.com, the Rhode Island Historical Cemetery Database, as well as Civil War veteran burial locations of the Sons of Union Veterans of the Civil War. Furthermore, the Veterans Affairs National Cemetery database was also utilized. No doubt, many of these men who were killed in action or who died of illness in the South will forever rest in a National Cemetery under a stone marked "Unknown." A cenotaph is a memorial marker in a cemetery in Rhode Island, the soldier's body remains buried in the South.

The result of this intense research was the location and identification of the burial locations of nearly two thirds of the men who served in the regiment. In addition, historic cemetery records located in each town hall in Rhode Island were also utilized. Furthermore, this author has personally visited nearly every cemetery in Rhode Island and has visited many of the graves recorded in these pages, confirming the identity of the man buried there as a member of the Fourth Rhode Island Volunteers. Also, details from George H. Allen's *Forty-Six Months with the Fourth Rhode Island* have also been used for the men of Company B.

Each man is identified, followed by the residence he claimed to hail from on the enlistment form. His age upon enlistment is also given, as is his marital status upon enlistment, designated by an "S" for single or "M" for married. Furthermore, his occupation is noted. Recruited from all over Rhode Island, the Fourth represented every walk of life in Civil War era New England. In addition, significant milestones in the soldier's life such as when and how they died or were injured in action, died of disease, discharged for disability, mustered out, or transferred to other organizations is noted.

It is important to note the men who died of disease or wounds after they were mustered out or discharged from the service due to disability and are not listed elsewhere as officially dying in the service; these men died as a direct result of their military service and are recorded here as such.

Unless otherwise noted, all members of the Fourth Rhode Island were mustered into Federal service for a period of three years on September 30, 1861.

When a soldier was promoted to become a non-commissioned officer such as a corporal or sergeant, he was promoted within his own company, however when he became a commissioned officer, he was almost universally sent to another company. Please follow the promotion progression of these men by referring to the text to see what company they were sent to after promotion. The final fate of each soldier and their burial location is listed under their final assignment in the Fourth Rhode Island.

For the sake of brevity, the following abbreviations are used in the register:

CIA: Captured in action

Co: Company

DOW: Died of wounds

KIA: Killed in action

MWIA: Mortally Wounded in Action

Trans: Transferred

USCT: U.S. Colored Troops

VRC: Veterans Reserve Corps

WIA: Wounded in action

The following is used to denote rank

Pvt: Private

Wag: Wagoner

Mus: Musician

Corp: Corporal

Sgt: Sergeant

1st Sgt: First Sergeant

Sgt. Maj: Sergeant Major

2nd Lt: Second Lieutenant

1st Lt: First Lieutenant

Capt: Captain

Maj: Major

Lt. Col: Lieutenant Colonel

Col: Colonel

Gen: General

Bvt: Brevet

    In regards to the residence of the soldier, the residence is that claimed upon the enlistment form, or when not listed, where the soldier last knowingly resided. In the case of Woonsocket, it should be noted for the record that Woonsocket did not officially exist as a separate town until 1867. In 1862, the village of Woonsocket consisted of a large industrial area comprising both the towns of Smithfield on the west bank of the Blackstone River, and Cumberland on the east side. It is nearly impossible to determine which side of the river a soldier may have resided on. As many soldiers claimed the then unincorporated village of Woonsocket as their home, it is listed in this roster as a separate place of residence then Cumberland and Smithfield. Furthermore, in 1861, the village of Fall River was still a part of the Town of Tiverton, Rhode Island. In 1862, Fall River became a city in Massachusetts, and Rhode Island gained the land that became East Providence. In addition, Smithfield was a much larger town at the time, and included what is now Woonsocket, North Smithfield, Lincoln, Central Falls, and the present Smithfield. Other Rhode Island boundaries have changed over time as well; readers are advised to consult the wonderful book *Rhode Island Boundaries: 1636-1936* by John Hutchins Cady.

This register is the result of over fifteen years and *countless* hours of study and revision. It will stand the test of time as the most complete and accurate record of a Rhode Island regiment during the Civil War. The men who served in the Fourth Rhode Island Volunteers did their duty to free the slave and preserve the Republic. I hope I have done their memory justice in preserving an accurate record of their name and deeds for posterity.

FIELD AND STAFF

Colonels

McCarthy, Justus I. Residence, New York, NY. 45. M. Soldier. Commissioned Sept. 30, 1861. Resigned Oct. 30, 1861. Died June 8, 1881. Interred at Oak Hill Cemetery, Washington, DC.

Rodman, Isaac Peace. Promoted from Lt. Col. Oct. 30, 1861. WIA Mar. 14, 1862 at New Bern, NC. Promoted to Brig. Gen. April 28, 1862. MWIA, shot in chest, Sept. 17, 1862 at Antietam, MD. DOW Sept. 30, 1862 at Sharpsburg, MD. Interred at Rodman Lot, South Kingstown Cemetery 30, South Kingstown, RI.

Steere, William H. P. Residence, Providence. 44. M. Merchant Promoted from Lt. Col. 2nd R.I. Vols. Aug. 11, 1862. WIA, shot in thigh, Sept. 17, 1862 at Antietam, MD. Mustered out Oct. 15, 1864. Bvt. Brig. Gen. Mar. 13, 1865 for "gallant and meritorious services." Died Aug. 25, 1882. Interred at North Burial Ground, Providence, RI.

Lieutenant Colonels

Buffum, Martin P. Promoted from Maj. Dec. 24, 1862. CIA July 30, 1864 at the Crater, Petersburg, VA. Mustered out Dec. 17, 1864. Bvt. Col. for actions at the Crater Mar. 13, 1865. After war joined United States Army and on April 20, 1884 "committed suicide in Texas, by reason of dissipation," also known as post-traumatic stress disorder, based on Civil War service.

Curtis, Joseph B. Promoted from Assistant Adjutant General (Capt.) staff of Gen. I.P. Rodman, Aug. 11, 1862. KIA Dec. 13, 1862 at Fredericksburg, VA. Interred at North Burial Ground, Providence, RI.

Rodman, Isaac Peace. Residence, South Kingstown. M. 40. Mill Owner. Promoted from Capt. Co. E, 2nd R.I. Vols. Sept. 30, 1861. Promoted to Col. Oct. 30, 1861.

Tew, George W. Promoted from Maj. Nov. 20, 1861. Resigned Aug. 11, 1862. Died Nov. 11, 1884. Interred at Island Cemetery, Newport, RI.

Majors

Allen, John A. Promoted from Capt. Co. E, Nov. 11, 1861. Resigned Aug. 11, 1862. Died Nov. 25, 1906. Interred at Woodland Cemetery, Quincy, IL.

Bucklin, James T.P. Promoted from Capt. Co. H, Jan. 9, 1863. Mustered out Oct. 15, 1864. Bvt. Col. Mar. 13, 1864. Died April 8, 1919. Interred at Swan Point Cemetery, Providence, RI.

Buffum, Martin P. Promoted from Capt. Co. B, Oct. 10, 1862. Promoted to Lt. Col. Dec. 24, 1862.

Kent, Levi E. Promoted from Capt. Co. F, Aug. 11, 1862. Resigned Sept. 26, 1862.

Tew, George W. Promoted from Capt. Co. G, Oct. 30, 1861. Promoted to Lt. Col. Nov. 11, 1861.

Adjutants

Curtis, Joseph B. Residence, Providence. 26. S. Engineer. Commissioned Oct. 30, 1861. WIA Mar. 14, 1862 at New Bern, NC. Promoted to Capt. and Assistant Adjutant General, staff of Brig. Gen. I. P. Rodman, June 9, 1862.

Spooner, Henry J. Promoted from 1st Lt. Co. E, Nov. 1, 1862. Trans. to 7th R.I. Vols. as regimental adjutant Oct. 21, 1864. Died Feb. 9, 1918. Interred at Swan Point Cemetery, Providence, RI.

Regimental Quartermasters

Knight, Brayton. Promoted from Commissary Sergeant, Nov. 25, 1862. Mustered out Oct. 15, 1864. Died of disease contracted in the service, June 15, 1865 at Warwick, RI. Interred at Stephen Knight Lot, Cranston Cemetery 91, Cranston, RI.

Smith, Charles S. Residence, Providence. 32. M. Commissioned Oct. 30, 1861. Resigned Aug. 11, 1862. Died Aug. 12, 1907. Interred at Swan Point Cemetery, Providence, RI.

Surgeon

Rivers, Henry W. Residence, Providence. 47. M. Doctor. Commissioned Oct. 30, 1861. Detached as Brigade Surgeon Mar. 8, 1862 and spent most of the war on medical staff duty. Mustered out Aug. 25, 1864. Died Dec. 3, 1868. Interred at North Burial Ground, Providence, RI.

Assistant Surgeons

Dedrick, Albert C. Residence, Providence. 30. M. Doctor. Commissioned Oct. 2, 1862. Mustered out Nov. 2, 1864. Died April 16, 1898. Interred at Centerville Methodist Cemetery, West Warwick Cemetery 11, West Warwick, RI.

Millar, Robert. Residence, Warwick. 28. M. Doctor. Commissioned Oct. 30, 1861. Mustered out Aug. 26, 1864. Died Dec. 17, 1909. Interred at Swan Point Cemetery, Providence, RI.

Smalley, George L. Residence, Coventry. 25. M. Doctor. Commissioned July 30, 1862. Discharged for disability Sept. 24, 1862. Died of disease contracted in the service, Nov. 23, 1862 at Providence, RI. Interred at Mt. Wollaston Cemetery, Quincy, MA.

Chaplains

Cummings, Silas S. Residence, Burrillville. 47. M. Minister. Commissioned Jan. 7, 1863. Resigned Oct. 11, 1863. Died Feb. 22, 1870. Interred at Riverside Cemetery, Lewiston, ME.

Flanders, Alonzo B. Residence, North Kingstown. 33. M. Minister. Commissioned Sept. 11, 1861. Resigned Oct. 31, 1862. Died April 5, 1898. Interred at Dellwood Cemetery, Manchester, VT.

Sergeant Majors

Drohan, John E. Residence, Warwick. 25. S. Carpenter. Enlisted Oct. 4, 1861. Promoted to 2nd Lt. Co. A, April 30, 1862.

Johnson, Edwin R. Promoted from Sgt. Co. H, June 29, 1862. Promoted to 2nd Lt. Co. A, Jan. 13, 1863.

Kibby, George L. Promoted from Sgt. Co. C, Jan. 13, 1863. Promoted to 2nd Lt. Co. D, Sept. 26, 1863.

Phillips, William A. Promoted from Sgt. Co. C, Sept. 23, 1863. Mustered out Oct. 15, 1864. Died 1898. Interred at Glenford Cemetery, Scituate, RI

Quartermaster Sergeants

Cummings, Silas W. Promoted from Corp. Co. E, Jan. 13, 1863. Mustered out Oct. 15, 1864. Died February 15, 1916. Interred at Swan Point Cemetery, Providence, RI.

Jenckes, Allen. Promoted from Wag. Co. E, Dec. 12, 1861. Promoted to 2nd Lt. Co. D, Jan. 12, 1863.

Smith, Zerah B. Residence, Providence. Merchant. Enlisted Oct. 30, 1861. Promoted to 2nd Lt. Co. I, Nov. 20, 1861.

Commissary Sergeants

Knight, Brayton. Residence, Warwick. 35. M. Grocer. Enlisted Sept. 17, 1861. Promoted to Regt. QM Nov. 25, 1862.

Nottage, Charles H. Promoted from Sgt. Co. H, Nov. 25, 1862. Mustered out Oct. 15, 1864. Died Feb. 11, 1896. Interred at Elm Grove Cemetery, North Kingstown, RI.

Hospital Steward

Griffin, Thomas J. Residence, Providence. 23. Enlisted Sept. 10, 1861. Mustered out Oct. 15, 1864. Died 1911. Interred at North Burial Ground, Providence, RI.

Principal Musician

Smith, Albert J. Residence, Newport. 18. S. Musician. Enlisted Sept. 7, 1861. Trans. to Co. G, 7th R.I. Vols. Oct. 21, 1864. Mustered out July 13, 1865. Died Aug. 14, 1887. Interred at Common Burial Ground, Newport, RI.

REGIMENTAL BAND

Bishop, Edward G. Residence, Providence. 23. Musician. Enlisted Sept. 16, 1861. Mustered out Oct. 3, 1862. Died Aug. 29, 1870. Interred at St. Paul's Cemetery, Norwalk, CT.

Butterfield, Jabez. Residence, Smithfield. 24. Musician. Enlisted Sept. 16, 1861. Trans. to Co. E, Nov. 15, 1861.

Burrows, Isaac H. Residence, Providence. 23. Musician. Enlisted Sept. 16, 1861. Mustered out Aug. 16, 1862.

Coggeshall, Charles E. Residence, Providence. 31. Musician. Enlisted Sept. 16, 1861. Mustered out Oct. 3, 1862. Died Mar. 28, 1880. Interred at Hope Cemetery, Worcester, MA.

Douglas, Oscar F. Residence, Providence. 19. Musician. Enlisted Sept. 16, 1861. Mustered out Oct. 3, 1862. Died Mar. 1, 1924. Interred at Oak Grove Cemetery, Fall River, MA.

Folger, Charles F. Residence, Providence. 27. Musician. Enlisted Sept. 16, 1861. Mustered out Oct. 3, 1862. Died July 5, 1905. Interred at Rural Cemetery, New Bedford, MA.

Gladding, Daniel P. Residence, Providence. 18. Musician Enlisted Sept. 16, 1861. Mustered out Oct. 3, 1862. Died Dec. 12, 1915. Interred at Forest Hill Cemetery, Fitchburg, MA.

Greene, Joseph C. Residence, Providence. 41. Musician. Appointed Band Leader. Enlisted Sept. 16, 1861. Mustered out Oct. 3, 1862. Died Dec. 23, 1891. Interred at North Burial Ground, Providence, RI.

Guinness, John. Residence, Providence. 26. Musician. Enlisted Sept. 16, 1861. Mustered out Oct. 3, 1862. Died Aug. 1, 1883. Interred at Swan Point Cemetery, Providence, RI.

Hudson, David. Residence, Providence. 23. Musician. Enlisted Sept. 16, 1861. Mustered out Oct. 3, 1862. Died 1925. Interred at Oak Dell Cemetery, South Kingstown, RI.

Jennison, Joseph G. Residence, Providence. 41. Musician. Enlisted Sept. 16, 1861. Mustered out Oct. 3, 1862.

Johnson, William H. Residence, Providence. 41. Musician. Enlisted Sept. 16, 1861. Mustered out Oct. 3, 1862.

Jonge, Daniel. Residence, Providence. 41. Musician. Enlisted Sept. 16, 1861. Mustered out Oct. 3, 1862.

Lavallee, Calixa. Residence, Providence. 21. S. Musician. Enlisted Sept. 17, 1861.WIA, shot in leg, Sept. 17, 1862 at Antietam, MD. Mustered out Oct. 3, 1862. Died January 21, 1891. Interred at Cote des Neiges Cemetery, Montreal, Quebec, Canada.

Lavallee, George. Residence, Providence. 26. Musician. Enlisted Sept. 16, 1861. Mustered out Oct. 3, 1862. Died June 11, 1879. Interred at Ezra Ramsdell Lot, Scituate Cemetery 99, Scituate, RI.

Leach, John. Residence, Providence. 23. Musician. Enlisted Sept. 16, 1861. Mustered out Oct. 3, 1862.

McCormick, James. Residence, Providence. 40. Musician. Enlisted Sept. 16, 1861. Mustered out Oct. 3, 1862.

Nader, William. Residence, Providence. 31. Musician. Enlisted Sept. 16, 1861. Mustered out Oct. 3, 1862. Died April 5, 1931. Interred at Calvary Cemetery, Brockton, MA.

Nichols, William T. Residence, Providence.23. Musician. Enlisted Sept. 16, 1861. Mustered out Oct. 3, 1862. Died Mar. 26, 1895. Interred at Oak Hill Cemetery, Woonsocket, RI.

Shaw, Orrin G. Residence, Providence. 27. Musician. Enlisted Sept. 16, 1861. Mustered out Oct. 3, 1862.

COMPANY A

Captains

Brown, Jeremiah. Promoted from 1st Lt. Co. A, Nov. 20, 1861. Dismissed from the service Aug. 11, 1862 for insubordination. Died 1879. Interred at North Burial Ground, Providence, RI.

Shearman, Sumner U. Promoted from 1st Lt. Co. A, Mar. 2, 1863. CIA July 30, 1864 at the Crater, Petersburg, VA. Mustered out Dec. 8, 1864. Died Feb. 15, 1914. Interred at Woodbrook Cemetery, Woburn, MA.

First Lieutenants

Brown, Jeremiah. Residence, Providence. 21. Commissioned Oct. 30, 1861. Promoted to Capt. Co. A, Nov. 20, 1861.

Johnson, Charles R. Promoted from 2nd Lt. Co. I, Nov. 20, 1861. Resigned April 27, 1862.

Johnson, Edwin R. Promoted from 2nd Lt. Co. A, Sept. 8, 1863. Mustered out Oct. 15, 1864. Interred at Elm Grove Cemetery, North Kingstown, RI.

Shearman, Sumner U. Promoted from 2nd Lt. Co. A, Nov. 25, 1862. Promoted to Capt. Co. A, Mar. 2. 1863.

Second Lieutenants

Bucklin, James T.P. Residence, Providence. 25. Commissioned Sept. 12, 1861. Promoted to 1st Lt. Co. E, Nov. 20, 1861.

Drohan, John E. Promoted from Sgt. Maj. April 30, 1862. Resigned Aug. 11, 1862. Died April 4, 1915. Interred at St. Mary's Cemetery, Norwich, CT.

Johnson, Edwin R. Promoted from Sgt. Maj. Jan. 13, 1863. Promoted to 1st Lt. Co. A, Sept. 8, 1863.

Knowles, John K. Residence, South Kingstown. 30. S. Farmer. Commissioned Aug. 14, 1863. KIA, July 30, 1864 at the Crater, Petersburg, VA. Cenotaph at James Knowles Lot, South Kingstown Cemetery 32, South Kingstown, RI.

Lyon, James W. Residence, Providence. Commissioned Nov. 7, 1861. Promoted to 1st Lt. Co. B. April 30, 1862.

Shearman, Sumner U. Residence, Providence. 25. S. Lawyer. Commissioned Aug. 25, 1862. Promoted to 1st Lt. Co. A, Nov. 25, 1862.

First Sergeants

Baker, Otis A. Residence, Providence. 23. S. Mason. Enlisted Sept. 7, 1861. Promoted to 2nd Lt. Co. D, Nov. 20, 1861.

Mann, John. Promoted from Pvt. Nov. 20, 1861. WIA, shot in the side, July 30, 1864 at the Crater, Petersburg, VA. Mustered out Oct. 15, 1864.

Sergeants

Jones, Benjamin D. Promoted from Corp. Sept. 17, 1862. Discharged to accept promotion to 2nd Lt. 14th R.I. Heavy Artillery. Jan. 29, 1864. Died Mar. 5, 1875. Interred at Swan Point Cemetery, Providence, RI.

Langworthy, Thomas A. Promoted from Corp. KIA July 30, 1864 at the Crater, Petersburg, VA. Cenotaph at Elm Grove Cemetery, North Kingstown, RI.

McInnes, Hugh. Promoted from Pvt. WIA, right arm amputated, July 30, 1864 at the Crater, Petersburg, VA. Mustered out Oct. 15, 1864. Died Nov. 14, 1915. Interred at White Brook Cemetery, Richmond, RI.

McMahon, Thomas. Residence, Providence. 19. M. Carpenter. Enlisted Sept. 5, 1861. Mustered out Oct. 15, 1864.

Tillinghast, Albert G. Residence, Providence. 25. M. Sail Maker. Enlisted Sept. 11, 1861. Promoted to 1st Lt. Co. H, Nov. 1, 1862.

Tompkins, Franklin P. Residence, Providence. 28. M. Moulder. Enlisted Sept. 5, 1861. WIA, shot in hip, July 30, 1864 at the Crater, Petersburg, VA. Trans. to Co. G, 7th R.I. Vols. Oct. 21, 1864. Mustered out July 13, 1865. Died Feb. 4, 1896. Interred at Riverside Cemetery, Pawtucket, RI.

Wilson, Charles. Residence, New York, NY. 35. S. Saddler. Enlisted Sept. 11, 1861. WIA Sept. 17, 1862 at Antietam, MD. Promoted to 2nd Lt. Co. H, Jan. 13, 1863.

Corporals

Ash, Charles E. Promoted from Pvt. Trans. to VRC Nov. 28, 1863. Died Nov. 23, 1931. Interred at Braman Cemetery, Newport, RI.

Campbell, Patrick H. Residence, Providence. 25. S. Porter. Enlisted Sept. 5, 1861. Mustered out Oct. 15, 1864.

Coggeshall, Thomas J. L. Residence, Warwick. 20. S. Boatman. Enlisted Sept. 23, 1861. Trans. to Co. B, 7th R.I. Vols. Oct. 21, 1864. Mustered out July 13, 1865.

Grimwood, James. Residence, Providence. 19. S. Operative. Enlisted Sept. 5, 1861. KIA May 3, 1863 near Suffolk, VA.

Jones, Benjamin D. Residence, Providence. 21. S. Student. Enlisted Sept. 5, 1861. WIA, shot in foot, Sept. 17, 1862 at Antietam, MD. Promoted to Sgt. Sept. 17, 1862.

Leonard, George A. Residence, Providence. 29. S. Blacksmith. Enlisted Sept. 6, 1861. Trans. to Co. G, 7th R.I. Vols. Oct. 21,

1864. Mustered out July 13, 1865. Died Oct. 24, 1890. Interred at North Burial Ground, Providence, RI.

Langworthy, Thomas A. Residence, Hopkinton. 24. S. Manufacturer. Enlisted Sept. 5, 1861. WIA, shot in hip, Sept. 17, 1862 at Antietam, MD. Promoted to Sgt.

Kilton, Samuel. Residence, Newport. 19. S. Soldier. Enlisted Sept. 12, 1862. WIA, shot in foot, Sept. 17, 1862 at Antietam, MD. Trans to VRC Nov. 23, 1863.

Thomas, George A. Promoted from Pvt. Mustered out Oct. 15, 1864. Died 1911. Interred at Elm Grove Cemetery, North Kingstown, RI.

Worden, Thomas A. Promoted from Pvt. WIA, shot in hand, July 30, 1864 at the Crater, Petersburg, VA. Mustered out Oct. 15, 1864. Died 1916. Interred at Wood River Cemetery, Richmond, RI.

Musicians

Hunt, Benjamin D. Residence, Burrillville. 33. M. Painter. Enlisted Sept. 28, 1861. Trans. to Co. D, 7th R.I. Vols. Mustered out July 13, 1865. Died May 12, 1910. Interred at Harrisville Cemetery, Burrillville, RI.

Rourke, Walter. Residence, Providence. 18. S. Laborer. Enlisted Sept. 6, 1861. Trans. to Co. G, 7th R.I. Vols. Oct. 21, 1864. Mustered out July 13, 1865.

Wagoners

Kelley, William. Residence, Providence. 30. M. Teamster. Enlisted Sept. 19, 1861. Discharged for disability Sept. 30, 1862 at Providence, RI. Died Mar. 28, 1901. Interred at Togus National Cemetery, Augusta, ME. Grave 1665.

Staples, Lyman A. Residence, Cumberland. 18. S. Laborer. Enlisted Sept. 5, 1861. Discharged for disability Dec. 7, 1862 at Falmouth, VA.

Privates

Albro, Daniel. Residence, Newport. 42. M. Engineer. Enlisted Sept. 7, 1861. Mustered out Oct. 15, 1864. Interred at Island Cemetery, Newport, RI.

Ames, Samuel. Residence, Plainfield, CT. 26. M. Laborer. Enlisted Sept. 26, 1861. Mustered out Oct. 15, 1864. Died Mar. 4, 1915. Interred at North Burial Ground, Bristol, RI.

Ash, Charles E. Residence, Newport. 19. S. Clerk. Enlisted Oct. 1, 1861. Promoted to Corp.

Aylesworth, George W. Residence, Providence. 23. S. Moulder. Enlisted Sept. 5, 1861. Discharged for disability Sept. 28, 1862. Died Oct. 27, 1900. Interred at Locust Grove Cemetery, Providence, RI.

Aylesworth, Oliver S. Residence, Providence. 27. S. Teamster. Enlisted Sept. 5, 1861. Mustered out Oct. 15, 1864. Died Oct. 12, 1892. Interred at Locust Grove Cemetery, Providence, RI.

Barber, John F. Residence, Providence. 20. S. Gilder. Enlisted Sept. 5, 1861. Trans. to Co. G, 7th R.I. Vols. Oct. 21, 1864. Mustered out June 9, 1865. Interred at Island Cemetery, Newport, RI.

Bayne, John. Residence, Providence. 19. S. Laborer. Enlisted Sept. 5, 1861. Deserted May 15, 1864.

Beggan, Thomas. Residence, Providence. 26. M. Blacksmith. Enlisted Aug. 26, 1862. Deserted Oct. 4, 1864.

Bicknell, Thomas. Residence, Providence. 21. S. Brush Maker. Enlisted Sept. 6, 1861. Trans. to Co. G, 7th R.I. Vols. Oct. 21, 1864. Mustered out July 13, 1865.

Bowers, John C. Residence, Coventry. 33. M. Farmer. Enlisted Nov. 19, 1862. Discharged for disability April 1, 1863 at Providence, RI. Died Feb. 2, 1901. Interred at National Veterans Home Cemetery, Dayton, OH.

Brayman, John. Residence, Providence. 20. S. Operative. Enlisted Sept. 5, 1861. Trans. to Co. G, 7th R.I. Vols. Oct. 21, 1864. Mustered out July 13, 1865.

Briggs, Thomas. Residence, Providence. 24. S. Jeweler. Enlisted Sept. 5, 1861. WIA, shot in elbow, Sept. 17, 1862 at Antietam, MD. Discharged for disability, Mar. 5, 1863 at Baltimore, MD. Died Oct. 25, 1872. Interred at John Parker Lot, Scituate Cemetery 159, Scituate, RI.

Brown, Daniel. Residence, Concord, NH. 33. M. Farmer. Enlisted Sept. 5, 1861. Died of typhoid at New Bern, NC May 3, 1863.

Bumpus, Sullivan L. Residence, Rochester, MA. 29. S. Cooper. Enlisted Sept. 7, 1861. KIA Sept. 17, 1862 at Antietam, MD. Interred at Woodside Cemetery, Plymouth, MA.

Burdick, John R. Residence, Hopkinton. 19. S. Line Maker. Enlisted Sept. 6, 1861. Discharged for disability Aug. 19, 1862 at Fort Monroe, MD. Died Sept. 16, 1913. Interred at Westville Cemetery, New Haven, CT.

Burke, Michael. Residence, Providence. 19. S. Machinist. Enlisted Sept. 10, 1861. Mustered out Oct. 15, 1864.

Cain, Thomas. Residence, Providence. 19. S. Operative. Enlisted Sept. 5, 1861. Mustered out Oct. 15, 1864.

Carline, Patrick. Residence, Taunton, MA. 22. S. Shoemaker. Enlisted Sept. 5, 1861. Trans. to Co. G, 7th R.I. Vols. Oct. 21, 1864. Mustered out July 13, 1865.

Casey, Patrick. Residence, North Bridgewater, MA. 23. S. Shoemaker. Enlisted Sept. 7, 1861. M. Laborer. WIA, shot in leg, Sept. 17, 1862 at Antietam, MD. WIA, shot in hand, July 30, 1864 at the Crater, Petersburg, VA. Trans. to Co. G, 7th R.I. Vols. Oct. 21, 1864. Mustered out July 13, 1865.

Coakley, Thomas. Residence, Providence. 27. M. Operative. Enlisted Sept. 5, 1861. Mustered out Oct. 15, 1864. Died Nov. 9, 1923. Interred at St. Mary's Catholic Cemetery, Ansonia, CT.

Cobb, Daniel H. Residence, Plainfield, CT. 26. M. Laborer. Enlisted Sept. 5, 1861. Mustered out Oct. 15, 1864. Interred at Oakland Cemetery, Cranston, RI.

Collum, George. Residence, Middletown. 21. S. Farmer. Enlisted Aug. 4, 1862. KIA July 30, 1864 at the Crater, Petersburg, VA.

Colwell, Marcus. Residence, Providence. 19. S. Jeweler. Enlisted Sept. 7, 1861. Trans. to Co. G, 7th R.I. Vols. Oct. 21, 1864. Mustered out Aug. 25, 1865.

Cook, Isaac B. Residence, Tiverton. 19. S. Farmer. Enlisted Aug. 15, 1862. Trans. to Co. G, 7th R.I. Vols. Oct. 21, 1864. Died April 12, 1905. Interred at David Rounds Lot, Tiverton Cemetery 16, Tiverton, RI.

Conley, John. Residence, Worcester, MA. 31. S. Spinner. Enlisted Sept. 5, 1861. Discharged for disability Jan. 12, 1864 at Portsmouth, RI. Died June 29, 1897. Interred at Togus National Cemetery, Augusta, ME. Grave 1347.

Conners, Thomas. Residence, Providence. 22. M. Laborer. Enlisted Sept. 5, 1861. Mustered out Oct. 15, 1864. Interred at St. Ann's Cemetery, Cranston, RI.

Crothers, William. Residence, Providence. 21. S. Laborer. Enlisted Sept. 5, 1861. Discharged for disability Jan. 12, 1864.

Donnelly, Frank. Residence, Providence. 41. M. Laborer. Enlisted Sept. 6, 1861. Trans. to Co. G, 7th R.I. Vols. Oct. 21, 1864. Mustered out July 13, 1865.

Donnelly, James. Residence, Randolph, MA. 37. M. Laborer. Enlisted Sept. 8, 1861. Trans. to the VRC Dec. 16, 1863. Interred at St. Francis Cemetery, Pawtucket, RI.

Dugan, Patrick. Residence, Providence. 27. S. Boot Maker. Enlisted Sept. 5, 1861. Died of typhoid Aug. 15, 1862 at Fredericksburg, VA.

Dunn, Peter. Residence, Providence. 29. S. Spinner. Enlisted Sept. 5, 1861. Discharged for disability Dec. 15, 1861 at Washington, DC.

Durfee, William. Residence, Providence. 19. S. Baker. Enlisted, Sept. 7, 1861. Trans. to the Regular Army, Oct. 24, 1862. Interred at Island Cemetery, Newport, RI.

Earley, John. Residence, Providence. 40. M. Farmer. Enlisted Aug. 21, 1862. Trans. to Co. G, 7th R.I. Vols. Oct. 21, 1864. Mustered out July 13, 1865. Interred at St. Mary's Cemetery, Pawtucket, RI.

Edgars, Edward. Residence, Providence. 33. M. Painter. Enlisted Sept. 5, 1861. Died of tuberculosis June 4, 1864 at Portsmouth, RI. Interred at Locust Grove Cemetery, Providence, RI.

Eston, Smith. Residence, Burrillville. 18. S. Farmer. Enlisted Sept. 7, 1861. Discharged for disability Dec. 7, 1862 at Alexandria, VA.

Finnegan, Hugh. Residence, Warwick. 33. S. Laborer. Enlisted July 7, 1862. WIA, shot in hand, Sept. 17, 1862 at Antietam, MD. WIA, shot in head, July 30, 1864 at the Crater, Petersburg, VA. Trans. to Co. G, 7th R.I. Vols. Oct. 21, 1864.

Freeborn, John P. Residence, Newport. 23. S. Machinist. Enlisted Aug. 15, 1862. WIA May 3, 1863 near Suffolk, VA. Trans. to Co. G, 7th R.I. Vols. Mustered out at Washington, DC, July 5, 1865. Died 1917. Interred at Middletown Village Cemetery, Middletown, RI.

Gardiner, William H. Residence, Providence. 23. S. Clerk. Enlisted Sept. 21, 1861. Discharged for disability Nov. 4, 1862. Died of tuberculosis contracted in the service at Providence, RI, Dec. 24, 1862. Interred at Grace Church Cemetery, Providence, RI.

Gallagher, Patrick. Residence, Providence. 18. S. Operative. Accidentally killed at Point Lookout, MD, May 7, 1864.

Gavitt, Reynolds H.C. Residence, Providence. 18. S. Laborer. Enlisted Aug. 7, 1862. Trans. to Co. G, 7th R.I. Vols. Oct. 21, 1864. Mustered out July 13, 1865. Interred at Wood River Cemetery, Richmond, RI.

Gilfoil, Patrick. Residence, Providence. 24. S. Farmer. Enlisted Sept. 7, 1861.WIA Sept. 17, 1862 at Antietam, MD. MWIA and CIA July 30, 1864 at the Crater, Petersburg, VA. Released. DOW Mar. 3, 1865 at Annapolis, MD. Interred at Annapolis National Cemetery, Annapolis, MD. Section N, Grave 120.

Griffin, William. Residence, North Bridgewater, MA. 24. S. Shoemaker. Enlisted Sept. 5, 1861. Mustered out Oct. 15, 1864. Died Nov. 2, 1864 of typhoid contracted in the service at North Bridgewater, MA. Interred at North Bridgewater, MA.

Gorman, Morris. Residence, Milford, MA. 21. S. Shoemaker. Enlisted Sept. 5, 1861. Trans. to Co. G, 7th R.I. Vols. Mustered out July 13, 1865.

Hopkins, Leonard. Residence, Johnston. RI. 24. S. Painter. Enlisted Sept. 5, 1861. Mustered out Oct. 15, 1864. Died Feb. 2, 1908. Interred at Glenford Cemetery, Scituate, RI.

Hodson, Robert. Residence, Warwick. 33. M. Painter. Enlisted, Sept. 7, 1861. Trans. to Co. G, 7th R.I. Vols. Mustered out July 13, 1865.

Holland, William H. Residence, Newport. 23. S. Blacksmith. Enlisted Sept. 5, 1861. Mustered out Oct. 15, 1864.

Hughes, Robert. Residence, Johnston. 21. S. Laborer. Enlisted Sept. 5, 1861. Deserted Sept. 13, 1862 near Middletown, MD.

Johnson, Henry E. Residence, Charlestown. 19. S. Laborer. Enlisted Sept. 5, 1861. Discharged for disability Nov. 20, 1862 at Washington, DC.

Johnson, Philip. Residence, Providence. 39. S. Soldier. Enlisted Sept. 5, 1861. KIA Mar. 14, 1862 at New Bern, NC.

Jones, Thomas. Residence, Providence. 27. S. Sailor. Enlisted Sept. 5, 1861. Trans. to VRC May 7, 1864.

Jordan, Andrew. Residence, Taunton, MA. 19. S. Laborer. Enlisted Sept. 5, 1861. Discharged for disability Dec. 3, 1862 at New York, NY. Died 1932. Interred at Pocasset Cemetery, Cranston, RI.

Jordan, Benjamin. Residence, Plainfield, CT. 26. S. Laborer. Enlisted, Sept. 28, 1861. Mustered out Oct. 15, 1864. Interred at Wood River Cemetery, Richmond, RI.

Keogh, John. Residence, Providence. 50. M. Block cutter. Enlisted Sept. 5, 1861. Mustered out Oct. 15, 1864.

Lewis, John B. Residence, Exeter. 25. S. Laborer. Enlisted Sept. 5, 1861. Deserted Sept. 13, 1862 near Frederick, MD. Died 1877. Interred at Moshassuck Cemetery, Central Falls, RI.

Locklin, John. Residence, Warwick. 24. S. Weaver. Enlisted Sept. 7, 1861. Mustered out Oct. 15, 1864.

Lyons, Thomas. Residence, East Greenwich. 50. S. Laborer. Enlisted Sept. 5, 1861. Died of typhoid at Falmouth, VA, Dec. 19, 1862.

McFarland, John N. Residence, Cranston. 23. S. Shoemaker. Enlisted Sept. 11, 1861. Died of tuberculosis at Cranston, RI, Feb. 13, 1862.

McInnes, Hugh. Residence, Richmond. 25. S. Carpenter. Enlisted Oct. 5, 1861. Promoted to Sgt.

McGee, Frank. Residence, New York, NY. 21. S. Laborer. Enlisted Sept. 7, 1861. Trans. to the Regular Army, Oct. 25, 1862.

Mann, John. Residence, Newport. 24. S. Sailor. Enlisted Sept. 20, 1861. Promoted to 1st Sgt Nov. 20, 1861.

Manning, Patrick. Residence, Providence. 29. M. Laborer. Enlisted Sept. 5, 1861. Trans. to Co. G, 7th R.I. Vols. Oct. 21, 1864. Mustered out July 13, 1865. Interred at St. Mary's Cemetery, Newport, RI.

Mauran, James. Residence, Providence. 22. S. Farmer. Enlisted Aug. 11, 1862. Mustered out Oct. 15, 1864.

Millington, John. Residence, Newport. 44. M. Minister. Enlisted Aug. 15, 1862. Discharged for disability Aug. 17, 1862 at Portsmouth, RI.

Murdock, John S. Residence, Plainfield, CT. 24. S. Painter. Enlisted Sept. 5, 1861. Mustered out Oct. 15, 1864.

Murlee, John. Residence, Providence. 22. S. Laborer. Enlisted Sept. 17, 1861. Discharged for disability Dec. 7, 1862 at Falmouth, VA

Murphy, James. Residence, New Bedford, MA. 21. S. Laborer. Enlisted Sept. 5, 1861. Trans. to Co. G, 7th R.I. Vols. Oct. 21, 1865.

Norris, Henry G. Residence, Boston, MA. 18. S. Soldier. Enlisted Sept. 7, 1861. Mustered out Oct. 15, 1864.

O'Mara, Thomas. Residence, North Bridgewater, MA. 21. S. Shoemaker. Enlisted Sept. 5, 1861. KIA at Elizabeth City, NC, Feb. 16, 1862.

Potter, Philip J. Residence, Westerly. 18. S. Sailor. CIA July 30, 1864 at the Crater, Petersburg, VA. Mustered out Oct. 15, 1864.

Riley, William. Residence, Providence. 44. M. Carpenter. Enlisted Sept. 5, 1861. Deserted Nov. 28, 1861 near Bladensburg, MD.

Rathbun, Larkin W. Residence, Exeter. 32. S. Farmer. Enlisted Sept. 5, 1861. Died of typhoid Mar. 21, 1862 at Washington, DC. Interred at Soldiers Home National Cemetery, Washington, DC. Section H, Grave 4552.

Salisbury, George M. Residence, Pawtucket. 32. Residence, Sept. 5, 1861. M. Machinist. Enlisted Sept. 5, 1861. Trans. to Co. G, 7th R.I. Vols. Oct. 21, 1864. Mustered out July 13, 1865.

Sears, John P. Residence, Providence. 34. S. Silversmith. Enlisted Sept. 5, 1861. Mustered out Oct. 15, 1864.

Shakshaft, George. Residence, Coventry. 35. M. Weaver. Enlisted Aug. 15, 1862. MWIA, shot in chest, July 30, 1864 at the Crater, Petersburg, VA. DOW at New York, Aug. 18, 1864. Interred at St. Mary's Cemetery, West Warwick, RI.

Slocum, Charles S. Residence, Richmond. 24. M. Laborer. Enlisted Sept. 6, 1861. CIA July 30, 1864 at the Crater, Petersburg, VA. Mustered out at Providence, RI, Mar. 17, 1865. Interred at Riverbend Cemetery, Westerly, RI.

Sutton, Thomas. Residence, Scituate. 40. M. Operative. Enlisted Sept. 5, 1861. Discharged for disability Jan. 22, 1863 at Washington, DC. Died July 21, 1888. Interred at Oak Grove Cemetery, Pawtucket, RI.

Sutton, William. Residence, Scituate. 19. S. Operative. Enlisted Sept. 5, 1861. Mustered out Oct. 15, 1864. Died Dec. 15, 1917. Interred at Usquepaugh Cemetery, South Kingstown, RI.

Taft, Abbot E. Residence, Providence. 18. S. Student. Enlisted Sept. 5, 1861. Discharged for disability Dec. 22, 1862 at Washington, DC. Died Jan. 23, 1874. Interred at North Burial Ground, Providence, RI.

Tew, William C. Residence, Newport. 24. S. Laborer. Enlisted Sept. 19, 1861. Drowned Apr. 13, 1864 in Long Island Sound while returning from veteran furlough. Interred at Island Cemetery, Newport, RI.

Thomas, George A. Residence, North Kingstown. 21. Farmer. Enlisted Sept. 5, 1861. Promoted to Corp.

Vars, William D. Residence, Westerly. 18. S. Clerk. Enlisted Sept. 5, 1861. Discharged for disability May 21, 1863 at Providence, RI.

Ward, James. Residence, Providence. 22. S. Laborer. Enlisted Sept. 7, 1861.WIA, shot in shoulder, Sept. 17, 1862 at Antietam, MD. Discharged for disability Feb. 26, 1863 at Washington, DC. Interred at Old St. Mary's Cemetery, Pawtucket Cemetery 8, Pawtucket, RI.

Welsh, Daniel. Residence, Newport. 22. Enlisted Sept. 19, 1861. M. Mason. WIA, shot in back, July 30, 1864 at the Crater. Mustered out Oct. 15, 1864.

Wood, Horace B. Residence, Coventry. 19. S. Farmer. Enlisted Nov. 19, 1862. Trans. to Co. G, 7th R.I. Vols. Oct. 21, 1864. Mustered out July 13, 1865. Died Feb. 18, 1913. Interred at Nunica Cemetery, Nunica, MI.

Worden, Thomas A. Residence, Richmond. 23. S. Laborer. Enlisted Sept. 6, 1861. Promoted to Corp.

COMPANY B

Captains

Buffum, Martin P. Residence, Providence. 31. M. Merchant. Commissioned Sept. 5, 1861. Promoted to Maj. Oct. 10, 1862.

Greene, Charles H. Promoted from 1st Lt. Co. B, April 15, 1863. Mustered out Oct. 15, 1864. Died Jan. 9, 1902. Interred at Swan Point Cemetery, Providence, RI.

Joslyn, Erastus. Promoted from 1st Lt. Co. B, Dec. 8, 1862. Resigned Mar. 25, 1863. Died Aug. 6, 1981. Interred at St. James Cemetery, Woonsocket, RI.

First Lieutenants

Greene, Charles H. Promoted from 2nd Lt. Co. B, Nov. 20, 1861. Promoted to Capt. Co. B, April 15, 1863.

Joslyn, Erastus. Promoted from 2nd Lt. Co. C, Nov. 11, 1862. Promoted to Capt. Co. B, Dec. 8, 1862.

Lyon, James W. Promoted from 2nd Lt. Co. A, April 30, 1862. Promoted to Capt. Co. H, May 23, 1863.

Morse, Benjamin E. Promoted from 2nd Lt. Co. B, Mar. 2, 1863. Mustered out Oct. 15, 1864. Interred at Oakland Cemetery, Cranston, RI.

Second Lieutenants

Burdick, Albert N. Promoted from 1st Sgt. Co. K, Dec. 8, 1861. Resigned Aug. 11, 1862. Died Sept. 6, 1913. Interred at Island Cemetery, Newport, RI.

Costello, George B. Promoted from 1st Sgt. Co. C, July 30, 1864. Trans. to Co. B, 7th R.I. Vols. Oct. 21, 1864. Mustered out July 13, 1865. Died of tuberculosis contracted in the service at Providence, RI, July 21, 1868. Interred at North Burial Ground, Providence, RI.

Field, George W. Residence, Providence. 27. S. Merchant. Commissioned Feb. 5, 1863. KIA July 30, 1864 at the Crater, Petersburg, VA. Cenotaph at Swan Point Cemetery, Providence, RI.

Greene, Charles H. Residence, Woonsocket. 26. S. Merchant. Commissioned Sept. 5, 1861. Promoted to 1st Lt. Co. B, Nov. 20, 1861.

Morse, Benjamin E. Promoted from Sgt. Co. H, Aug. 11, 1862. Detached to ambulance train. Promoted to 1st Lt. Co. B, Mar. 2, 1863.

Pierce, Edwin A. Promoted from 1st Sgt. Co. E, Aug. 11, 1862. Promoted to 1st Lt. Co. G, Feb. 18, 1863.

First Sergeants

Cahoone, Calvin G. Promoted from Sgt. Oct. 1, 1861. Promoted to 2nd Lt. Co. C, Nov. 20, 1861.

Coon, Alphonzo. Promoted from Sgt. July 16, 1862. Discharged for disability Feb. 1, 1863.

Hughes, John. Residence, Providence. 30. S. Jeweler. Enlisted Sept. 5, 1861. Reduced to the ranks Oct. 1, 1861.

Preston, Samuel F. Promoted from Sgt. Feb. 1, 1863. Mustered out Oct. 15, 1864. Died Nov. 28, 1898. Interred at Oak Hill Cemetery, Woonsocket, RI.

Sergeants

Cahoone, Calvin G. Residence, Providence. 30. S. Jeweler. Enlisted Sept. 27, 1861. Promoted to 1st Sgt. Oct. 1, 1861.

Coon, Alphonzo. Residence, Hopkinton. 25. S. Farmer. Enlisted Sept. 5, 1861. Promoted to 1st Sgt. July 16, 1862.

Gray, Andrew T. Promoted from Corp. July 16, 1862. Discharged for disability Dec. 6, 1862. Died Nov. 6, 1899. Interred at Warsaw Cemetery, Warsaw, NY.

Gray, Stanton A. Residence, Providence. 27. S. Printer. Enlisted Sept. 5, 1862. Mustered out Oct. 15, 1864. Died Sept. 28, 1903. Interred at Locust Grove Cemetery, Providence, RI.

Hunt, Frederick A. Residence, Westerly. 21. S. Spinner. Enlisted Sept. 5, 1861. Reduced to the ranks.

McCann, Arthur. Promoted from Pvt. WIA, shot in leg, July 19, 1864 at Petersburg, VA. Mustered out Oct. 15, 1864. Died Mar. 12, 1898. Interred at St. Francis Cemetery, Pawtucket, RI.

Myrick, Cromwell P. Promoted from Pvt. MWIA July 17, 1864 in front of Petersburg, VA. DOW July 19, 1864 at City Point, VA. Interred at City Point National Cemetery, Hopewell, VA. Grave 1623. Cenotaph in Manchester Cemetery, Coventry, RI.

Preston, Samuel F. Residence, Providence. 30. M. Farmer. Enlisted Sept. 5, 1861. Promoted to 1st Sgt. Feb. 1, 1863.

Corporals

Allen, George H. Promoted from Pvt. Trans. to Co. B, 7th R.I. Vols. Oct. 21, 1864. Mustered out July 13, 1865. Died Sept. 5, 1895. Interred at North Burial Ground, Providence, RI.

Clarke, John R. Promoted from Pvt. July 16, 1862. Mustered out Oct. 15, 1864. Died 1928. Interred at White Brook Cemetery, Richmond, RI.

Gray, Andrew T. Residence, Providence. 19. S. Painted. Enlisted Sept. 5, 1861. Promoted to Sgt. July 16, 1862.

Hayberts, James. Residence, Providence. 32. M. Sailor. Enlisted Sept. 5, 1861. Reduced to the ranks.

Gorton, Reynolds. Promoted from Pvt. Nov. 15, 1861. Mustered out Oct. 15, 1864. Died Aug. 20, 1900. Interred at Knotty Oak Cemetery, Coventry, RI.

Greene, Benjamin C. Residence, Providence. 23. S. Painted. Enlisted Sept. 5, 1861. Reduced to the ranks Nov. 24, 1861.

Harvey, James F. Promoted from Pvt. Nov. 15, 1861. Trans to VRC May 10, 1864.

Harvey, Samuel. Promoted from Pvt. KIA Sept. 17, 1862 at Antietam, MD. Interred at Antietam National Cemetery, Sharpsburg, MD. Rhode Island Section, Grave 2842.

Larkham, Charles. Residence, Charlestown. 24. M. Clerk. Enlisted Sept. 5, 1861. Reduced to the ranks.

Perkins, Austin A. Residence, Richmond. 23. M. Laborer. Enlisted Sept. 5, 1861. WIA Feb. 10, 1862 at Roanoke, NC. KIA Sept. 17, 1862 at Antietam, MD.

Starkley, William B. Promoted from Pvt. Mustered out Oct. 15, 1864.

Wilcox, Willard P. Promoted from Pvt. Nov. 15, 1861. KIA Sept. 17, 1862 at Antietam, MD. Interred at Antietam National Cemetery, Sharpsburg, MD. Rhode Island Section, Grave 2821.

Musicians

Brown, Henry S. Residence, Exeter. 41. M. Laborer. Enlisted Sept. 5, 1861. Discharged for disability Jan. 20, 1863 at Falmouth, VA. Died Mar. 11, 1888. Interred at North Burial Ground, Providence, RI.

Card, Jonathan. Residence, South Kingstown. 44. M. Laborer. Enlisted Sept. 5, 1861. Died of typhoid, Mar. 1, 1862 at Roanoke, NC. Interred at New Bern National Cemetery, New Bern, NC. Section 11, Grave 1880. Cenotaph at Pine Grove Cemetery, Coventry, RI.

Wagoner

Bowen, Gilbert L. Residence, Providence. 22. M. Laborer. Enlisted Sept. 5, 1861. Mustered out Oct. 15, 1864. Died Nov. 21, 1908. Interred at Mineral Spring Cemetery, Pawtucket, RI.

Privates

Allen, George H. Residence, Providence. 24. M. Baker. Enlisted Sept. 6, 1861. Promoted to Corp.

Ambrose, George. Residence, Windsor, VT. 21. S. Farmer. Enlisted Dec. 20, 1862. Deserted Mar. 13, 1863 near Norfolk, VA.

Armes, Nicholas B. Residence, Providence. Enlisted Aug. 15, 1862. Trans. to Co. B, 7th R.I. Vols. Oct. 21, 1864. Mustered out June 9, 1865.

Arnold, Silas. Residence, Providence. 35. M. Miller. Enlisted Sept. 5, 1861. Discharged for disability Feb. 9, 1863 at Portsmouth, RI. Died May 8, 1888. Interred at Mineral Spring Cemetery, Pawtucket, RI.

Arnold, Thomas. Residence, Providence. 16. S. Laborer. Enlisted Sept. 29, 1861. Mustered out Oct. 15, 1864. Died Jan. 21, 1922. Interred at North Burial Ground, Providence, RI.

Bane, William H. Residence, Charlestown. 21. M. Carder. Enlisted Sept. 6, 1861. Died of typhoid, Jan. 4, 1862 at Alexandria, VA. Interred at Wood River Cemetery, Richmond, RI.

Bates, Albert E. Residence, Charlestown. 22. M. Weaver. Enlisted Sept. 5, 1861. Died of typhoid, Jan. 1, 1863 at Philadelphia, PA. Interred at Philadelphia National Cemetery, Philadelphia, PA. Section B. Grave 211.

Bates, George E. Residence, Providence. 22. M. Jeweler. Enlisted Sept. 5, 1861. Trans. to Co. B, 7th R.I. Vols. Oct. 21, 1864. Mustered out June 9, 1865. Died April 27, 1890. Interred at Swan Point Cemetery, Providence, RI.

Beers, Cyrus S. Residence, Ware, MA. 21. S. Farmer. Enlisted Sept. 12, 1861. WIA, shot in ankle, Sept. 17, 1862 at Antietam, MD. Discharged for disability Jan. 6, 1863 at Baltimore, MD. Died May 26, 1909. Interred at Nebraska Veterans Home, Grand Island, NE.

Bennett, George W. Residence, Providence. 42. S. Jeweler. Enlisted Aug. 15, 1862. Mustered out Oct. 15, 1864. Died May 6, 1881. Interred at Pine Grove Cemetery, Coventry, RI.

Bowdoin, Francis. Residence, Cranston. 33. S. Farmer. Enlisted Aug. 17, 1862. Discharged for disability Feb. 7, 1863.

Brown, Jonathan A. Residence, Cumberland. 34. M. Laborer. Enlisted Sept. 5, 1861. Mustered out Oct. 15, 1864. Died April 29, 1924. Interred at Angell-Eddy Lot, Foster Cemetery 57, Foster, RI.

Budlong, Charles R. Residence, Johnston. 27. S. Farmer. Enlisted Sept. 18, 1861. Mustered out Oct. 15, 1864. Died Feb. 26, 1890. Interred at Brayton Cemetery, Warwick, RI.

Burdick, Charles E. Residence, Newport. 19. S. Plumber. Enlisted Aug. 13, 1862. Trans. to Co. B, 7th R.I. Vols. Oct. 21, 1864. Mustered out June 9, 1865.

Burdick, Stephen H. Residence, South Kingstown. 35. M. Blacksmith. Enlisted Sept. 5, 1861. MWIA, shot in groin, Sept. 17, 1862 at Antietam, MD. DOW Sept. 27, 1862 at Sharpsburg, MD. Interred at Antietam National Cemetery, Sharpsburg, MD. Rhode Island Section, Grave 2822.

Burns, Timothy. Residence, Providence. 35. M. Tailor. Enlisted Sept. 5, 1861. Died of typhoid at Beaufort, NC June 17, 1862.

Card, Alvin L. Residence, Charlestown. 35. M. Miller. Enlisted Sept. 5, 1861. Mustered out Oct. 15, 1864. Died 1913. Interred at Pine Grove Cemetery, Hopkinton, RI.

Carey, Edward. Residence, Providence. 42. M. Laborer. Enlisted June 23, 1862. Trans. to Co. B, 7th R.I. Vols. Oct. 21, 1864. Mustered out June 9, 1865.

Cassiday, Patrick. Residence, Providence. Enlisted Nov. 18, 1862. Trans. to VRC Oct. 24, 1862.

Chapman, Amos P. Residence, Westerly. 21. S. Farmer. Enlisted Sept. 5, 1861. Discharged for disability July 27, 1862 at Newport News, VA. Died Dec. 30, 1925. Interred at River Bend Cemetery, Westerly, RI.

Chase, Artemus S. Residence, New Bedford, MA. Enlisted Sept. 13, 1861. Trans. to Co. B, 7th R.I. Vols. Oct. 21, 1864. Mustered out July 13, 1865. Died of disease contracted in the service at New Bedford, Massachusetts, Dec. 15, 1865.

Clarke, John R. Residence, Charlestown. 21. S. Farmer. Enlisted Sept. 5, 1861. Promoted to Corp. July 16, 1862.

Collins, Albert R. Residence, Providence. 27. M. Painter. Enlisted Sept. 5, 1861. Trans. to Co. B, 7th R.I. Vols. Oct. 21, 1864. Mustered out July 13, 1865. Died June 8, 1898. Interred at Spring Brook Cemetery, Mansfield, MA.

Coen, Martin. Residence, Providence. 36. M. Mason. Enlisted Sept. 18, 1861. Mustered out Oct. 15, 1864. Died July 6, 1884. Interred at Togus National Cemetery, Augusta, ME. Grave 292.

Congdon, John R. Residence, Providence. 45. M. Miller. Enlisted Sept. 7, 1861. Discharged for disability Dec. 16, 1861 at Washington, DC. Died Jan. 16, 1875. Interred at North Burial Ground, Providence, RI.

Cornell, Albert G. Residence, Coventry. 21. S. Machinist. Enlisted Sept. 7, 1861. Mustered out Oct. 15, 1864. Died 1917. Interred at Knotty Oak Cemetery, Coventry, RI.

Erwin, George. Residence, Cumberland. 18. S. Laborer. Enlisted Sept. 7, 1861. WIA, shot in left leg, May 3, 1863 near Suffolk, VA. Trans. to VRC Mar. 31, 1864. Died April 1, 1914. Interred at Oak Grove Cemetery, Pawtucket, RI.

Fiske, Charles L. Residence, Coventry. 25. S. Farmer. Enlisted Sept. 7, 1861. Mustered out Oct. 15, 1864. Died Sept. 19, 1906. Interred at Capt. Solomon Taylor Lot, Scituate Cemetery 81, Scituate, RI.

Fiske, Eugene. Residence, Providence. 24. S. Laborer. Enlisted April 19, 1864. Mustered in April 27, 1864. Mustered out July 13, 1865. Trans. to Co. B, 7th R.I. Vols. Oct. 21, 1864.

Ford, Stephen H. Residence, Scituate. 17. S. Farmer. Enlisted Sept. 7, 1861. Deserted in the face of the enemy Sept. 17, 1862 at Antietam, MD.

Gardiner, James A. Residence, North Kingstown. 20. M. Machinist. Enlisted Sept. 5, 1861. Discharged for disability Dec.

14, 1862. Died 1912. Interred at Elm Grove Cemetery, North Kingstown, RI.

Gardiner, William A. Residence, Providence. 35. M. Jeweler. Enlisted Sept. 5, 1861. Discharged for disability Dec. 14, 1861. Interred at Grace Church Cemetery, Providence, RI.

Gavin, John. Residence, Westerly. 24. S. Farmer. Enlisted Sept. 5, 1861. Deserted Sept. 6, 1862 near Washington, DC.

Gibson, Ephraim. Residence, Providence. 28. Enlisted Sept. 5, 1861. S. Farmer. Discharged for disability Mar. 4, 1863 at Portsmouth, RI

Gorton, Reynolds. Residence, Coventry. 19. S. Farmer. Enlisted Sept. 10, 1861. Promoted to Corp. Nov. 15, 1861.

Greene, Benjamin C. Reduced from Corp. Nov. 24, 1861. WIA, shot in leg, Sept. 17, 1862 at Antietam, MD. Discharged for disability Dec. 1, 1862. Interred at Oakland Cemetery, Cranston, RI.

Harvey, James F. Residence, Coventry. 21. S. Clerk. Enlisted Sept. 5, 1861. Promoted to Corp. Nov. 15, 1861.

Harvey, Samuel. Residence, Hopkinton. 28. S. Sailor. Enlisted Sept. 12, 1861. Promoted to Corp.

Hayberts, James. Reduced from Corp. Mustered out Oct. 15, 1864.

Healey, Reuben A. Residence, Westerly. 21. S. Farmer. Enlisted Sept. 5, 1861. WIA Mar. 14, 1862 at New Bern, NC. Discharged for disability Dec. 9, 1862 at Providence, RI. Died Mar. 14, 1924. Interred at Cross Mills Cemetery, Charlestown, RI.

Holloway, Elisha J. Residence, Charlestown. 28. S. Farmer. Enlisted Sept. 13, 1861. WIA, shot in shoulder, Sept. 17, 1862 at Antietam, MD. Discharged for disability Dec. 10, 1862 at

Providence, RI. Died 1897. Interred at Clarke-Webster Lot, Charlestown Cemetery 46, Charlestown, RI.

Hopkins, Allen. Residence, Glocester. 30. M. Farmer. Enlisted Sept. 6, 1861. KIA Sept. 17, 1862 at Antietam, MD. Interred at Smithville Cemetery, Scituate, RI.

Hughes, John. Reduced from 1st Sgt. Discharged for disability Mar. 13, 1863. Died Oct. 12, 1896. Interred at North Burial Ground, Providence, RI.

Hunt, Frederick A. Reduced from Sgt. Deserted in the face of the enemy Sept. 17, 1862 at Antietam, MD. Died Nov. 28, 1877. Interred at Oak Grove Cemetery, Hopkinton, RI.

Jefferson, James W. Residence, Boston. 24. S. Tailor. Enlisted Dec. 23, 1862. Died of typhoid Feb. 6, 1863 at Falmouth, VA.

Johnson, Elijah. Residence, East Greenwich. 20. S. Farmer. Enlisted Sept. 5, 1861. KIA Sept. 17, 1862 at Antietam, MD.

Keech, David. Residence, Westerly. 24. S. Farmer. Enlisted Sept. 5, 1861. WIA Mar. 14, 1862 at New Bern, NC. Deserted while under confinement at Beaufort, NC, July 6, 1862.

Kelley, Daniel. Residence, Warren. 29. S. Machinist. Enlisted Sept. 5, 1861. Dishonorably discharged by order of court martial May 10, 1864. Died Jan. 16, 1886. Interred at North Burial Ground, Providence, RI.

Kentworthy, Robert. Residence, Cumberland. 31. M. Machinist. Enlisted Sept. 5, 1861. KIA Mar. 14, 1862 at New Bern, NC.

Kinney, James. Residence, Hopkinton. 31. M. Farmer. Enlisted Sept. 23, 1861. Trans. to Co. B, 7th R.I. Vols. Oct. 21, 1864. Mustered out July 13, 1865. Interred at Wood River Cemetery, Richmond, RI.

Larkham, Charles. Reduced from Corp. Mustered out Oct. 15, 1864. Died Mar. 13, 1916. Interred at First Cemetery, East Greenwich, RI.

Livsey, John. Residence, Providence. 36. M. Weaver. Enlisted Sept. 5, 1861. Discharged for disability Dec. 6, 1862. Died 1882. Interred at Greenwood Cemetery, Coventry, RI.

Luther, George P. Residence, Providence. 20. S. Student. Enlisted Sept. 27, 1861. Mustered out Oct. 15, 1864.

McCann, Arthur. Residence, Providence. 23. S. Laborer. Enlisted Sept. 5, 1861. WIA May 3, 1863 near Suffolk, VA. Promoted to Sgt.

McDonald, Edward. Residence, Coventry. 30. M. Laborer. Enlisted Sept. 5, 1861. Detached on staff of Gen. O.O. Howard. Died of disease July 7, 1864 at Nashville, TN. Interred at Nashville National Cemetery, Nashville, TN. Section H, Grave 10069. Cenotaph at Pine Grove Cemetery, Coventry, RI.

McNeal, Patrick. Residence, Johnston. 28. S. Farmer. Enlisted Sept. 5, 1861. KIA Sept. 17, 1862 at Antietam, MD. Interred at Antietam National Cemetery, Sharpsburg, MD. Rhode Island Section, Grave 2832.

Matthewson, Rhodes S. Residence, Coventry. 21. S. Farmer. Enlisted Sept. 7, 1861. WIA Mar. 14, 1862 at New Bern, NC. Mustered out Oct. 15, 1864. Died 1913. Interred at Knotty Oak Cemetery, Coventry, RI.

Moon, Jeremiah. Residence, Coventry. 23. S. Farmer. Enlisted Sept. 5, 1861. Mustered out Oct. 15, 1864. Interred at Knotty Oak Cemetery, Coventry, RI.

Moon, Josiah. Residence, Coventry. 23. M. Farmer. Enlisted Sept. 5, 1861. KIA Sept. 17, 1862 at Antietam, MD. Interred at Antietam National Cemetery, Sharpsburg, MD. Rhode Island Section, Grave 2829.

Myrick, Cromwell P. Residence, Coventry. 22. S. Laborer. Enlisted Sept. 5, 1861. Promoted to Sgt.

Myrick, Samuel. Residence, Coventry. 30. M. Painter. Enlisted Sept. 5, 1861. KIA Mar. 14, 1862 at New Bern, NC. Interred at Greenwood Cemetery, Coventry, RI.

Myrick, Solomon. Residence, Coventry. 27. S. Laborer. Enlisted Sept. 5, 1861. Mustered out Oct. 15, 1864. Interred at Oakland Cemetery, Cranston, RI.

Newman, William. Residence, Westerly. 18. S. Carder. Enlisted Sept. 6, 1861. Mustered out Oct. 15, 1864.

Oliver, Joseph. Residence, Providence. 43. S. Shoemaker. Enlisted Sept. 5, 1861. KIA Sept. 17, 1862 at Antietam, MD.

Plunkett, Christopher. Residence, Providence. 24. M. Laborer. Enlisted Sept. 5, 1861. WIA, shot in leg and amputated, July 17, 1864 at Petersburg, VA. Mustered out Oct. 15, 1864. Interred at St. Mary's Cemetery, Pawtucket, RI.

Preston, George W. Residence, Coventry. 30. S. Laborer. Enlisted Sept. 5, 1861. WIA, shot in neck, Sept. 17, 1862 at Antietam, MD. Trans. to Co. B, 7th R.I. Vols. Oct. 21, 1864. Mustered out July 29, 1865. Died Oct. 22, 1867. Interred at Moshassuck Cemetery, Central Falls, RI.

Randall, James H. Residence, Providence. 31. M. Moulder. Enlisted Sept. 5, 1861. Died of small pox Mar. 12, 1864 at Portsmouth, VA. Interred at Hampton National Cemetery, Section B, Grave 4662. Cenotaph at Intervale Cemetery, North Providence, RI.

Randall, Luther R. Residence, Residence, Providence. 33. M. Teamster. Enlisted Aug. 15, 1862. WIA May 3, 1863 at Suffolk, VA. Trans. to Co. B, 7th R.I. Vols. Oct. 21, 1864. Mustered out

June 9, 1865. Died June 3, 1880. Interred at North Burial Ground, Providence, RI.

Ready, John. Residence, Providence. 21. S. Laborer. Enlisted Sept. 5, 1861. Died of dysentery Jan. 25, 1862 at Hatteras, NC.

Reynolds, Joseph J. Residence, Exeter. 19. S. Farmer. Enlisted Sept. 13, 1861. WIA, shot in thigh, Sept. 17, 1862 at Antietam, MD. Discharged for disability Dec. 18, 1862 at Providence, RI.

Richmond, Ferdinand. Residence, Coventry. 31. Laborer. Enlisted Sept. 5, 1861. Discharged for disability Jan. 30, 1863 at Alexandria, VA. Died Dec. 29, 1868. Interred at Pine Grove Cemetery, Coventry, RI.

Roberts, Henry. Residence, Providence. 18. S. Jeweler. Enlisted Sept. 5, 1861. KIA Sept. 17, 1862 at Antietam, MD. Interred in unknown grave, Antietam National Cemetery, Sharpsburg, MD.

Roe, Jacob. Residence, Johnston. 30. M. Laborer. Enlisted Sept. 5, 1861. KIA Sept. 17, 1862 at Antietam, MD.

Sabine, Silas. Residence, Voluntown, CT. 18. S. Farmer. Enlisted Sept. 5, 1861. CIA July 30, 1864 at the Crater, Petersburg, VA. Mustered out Nov. 30, 1864. Died Jan. 14, 1891. Interred at Enos-Crandall Lot, Hopkinton Cemetery 36, Hopkinton, RI.

Saunders, Stephen H. Residence, Providence. 30. S. Jeweler. Enlisted Sept. 5, 1861. Mustered out Oct. 15, 1864.

Sheldon, David A. Residence, Johnston. 18. S. Farmer. Enlisted Sept. 7, 1861. Trans. to Co. B, 7th R.I. Vols. Oct. 21, 1864. Mustered out July 13, 1865. Died 1915. Interred at Plainland Cemetery, Coventry, RI.

Sherman, Abial. Residence, Exeter. S. Farmer. Enlisted Sept. 5, 1861. Mustered out Oct. 15, 1864. Died June 20, 1889. Interred at Wood River Cemetery, Richmond, RI.

Small, Edwin M. Residence, Smithfield. 18. S. Farmer. Enlisted Sept. 16, 1861. Mustered out Oct. 15, 1864.

Starkley, William B. Residence, Providence. 26. M. Painter. Enlisted Sept. 5, 1861. Promoted to Corp.

Sullivan, Charles E. Residence, Charlestown. 29. M. Laborer. Enlisted Sept. 6, 1861. Mustered out Oct. 15, 1864. Interred at White Brook Cemetery, Richmond, RI.

Thornton, Augustus F. Residence, Dedham, MA. 22. S. Painter. Enlisted Sept. 5, 1861. KIA July 30, 1864 at the Crater, Petersburg, VA.

Thayer, William T. Residence, Smithfield. 45. S. Farmer. Enlisted Nov. 3, 1862. Trans. to Co. B, 7th R.I. Vols. Oct. 21, 1864. Mustered out July 13, 1865.

Turner, Charles E. Residence, Coventry. 18. S. Farmer. Enlisted Sept. 5, 1861. Discharged for disability Jan. 30, 1863 at Alexandria, VA. Interred at Greenwood Cemetery, Coventry, RI.

Turner, James. Residence, Westerly. 21. S. Painter. Enlisted Sept. 5, 1861. Discharged for disability May 30, 1862 at Alexandria, VA. Interred at Riverbend Cemetery, Westerly, RI.

Tyson, George. Residence, Providence. 35. M. Laborer. Enlisted Sept. 5, 1861. Discharged for disability Dec. 13, 1862 at Providence, RI.

Waterman, George G. Residence, Johnston. 18. S. Laborer. Enlisted July 25, 1864. Trans. to Co. B, 7th R.I. Vols. Oct. 21, 1864. Mustered out July 13, 1865. Died July 26, 1936. Interred at Lakeside-Carpenter Cemetery, East Providence, RI.

Waterman, William A. Residence, Providence. 26. M. Laborer. Enlisted Sept. 5, 1861. Trans. to Co. B, 7th R.I. Vols. Oct. 21, 1864. Mustered out July 13, 1865. Died Feb. 25, 1900. Interred at St. Ann Cemetery, Cranston, RI.

West, William B. Residence, Newport. 29. M. Mason. Enlisted Aug. 15, 1862. Trans. to the U.S. Navy, May 12, 1864. Died Jan. 17, 1910. Interred at Common Burial Ground, Newport, RI.

Westgate, Edwin W. Residence, Warren. 30. M. Laborer. Enlisted Sept. 5, 1861. Mustered out Oct. 15, 1864. Interred at Pine Grove Cemetery, Waterboro, ME.

Whitehead, Uriah. Residence, Johnston. 23. S. Spinner. Enlisted Sept. 5, 1861. Mustered out Oct. 15, 1864. Died Jan. 3, 1911. Interred at Togus National Cemetery, Augusta, ME. Grave 2812.

Wilcox, Willard P. Residence, Coventry. 23. M. Laborer. Enlisted Sept. 5, 1861. Promoted to Corp. Nov. 15, 1861.

Wilson, Joseph. Residence, Providence. 34. M. Enlisted Oct. 3, 1863. Trans. to Co. D, 7th R.I. Vols. Oct. 21, 1864. Mustered out July 13, 1865. Died Sept. 23, 1896. Interred at North Burial Ground, Providence, RI.

Williams, Archelus A. Residence, Providence. 18. S. Painter. Enlisted Sept. 5, 1861. Mustered out Oct. 15, 1864. Died of "heart disease" contracted in the service February 6, 1866, at Providence, RI.

Wilmarth, Nathan B. Residence, Providence. 24. S. Teamster. Enlisted Sept. 5, 1861. Mustered out Oct. 15, 1864

COMPANY C

Captains

Hall, William F. Promoted from 1st Lt. Co. F, Aug. 11, 1862. WIA, shot in leg, July 30, 1864 at the Crater, Petersburg, VA. Mustered out Oct. 15, 1864. Died July 7, 1906. Interred at North Burial Ground, Providence, RI.

Simon, Henry. Residence, Providence. 40. M. Jeweler. Commissioned Sept. 30, 1861. Resigned Aug. 11, 1862. Reentered service as captain in 14th R.I. Heavy Artillery 1863. Died Oct. 6, 1864. Interred at North Burial Ground, Providence, RI.

First Lieutenants

Cahoone, Calvin G. Promoted from 2nd Lt. Co. C, Dec. 20, 1861. Resigned July 30, 1862. Died June 14, 1874. Interred at Swan Point Cemetery, Providence, RI.

Waterman, George F. Promoted from 2nd Lt. Co. C, Sept. 15, 1863. Discharged for disability Sept. 19, 1864. Died Oct. 18, 1903. Interred at Oakland Cemetery, Cranston, RI.

West, Walter E. Promoted from 2nd Lt. Co. C, July 30, 1862. Resigned Aug. 11, 1862.

Second Lieutenants

Cahoone, Calvin G. Promoted from 1st Sgt. Co. B, Nov. 20, 1861. Promoted to 1st Lt. Co. C, Dec. 20, 1861.

Farley, James. H. Promoted from 1st Sgt. Co. C, April 11, 1864. KIA July 26, 1864 at Petersburg, VA. Interred at City Point National Cemetery, Hopewell, VA. Grave 2577.

Grinnell, James S. Promoted from Sgt. Co. H, Aug. 1, 1864. Mustered out Oct. 15, 1864. Died Feb. 26, 1873. Interred at Elm Grove Cemetery, North Kingstown, RI.

Hall, William F. Residence, Providence. Commissioned Sept. 30, 1861. Promoted to 1st Lt. Co. F, Oct. 11, 1861.

Joslyn, Erastus. Promoted from Sgt. Co. E, Nov. 20, 1861. Promoted to 1st Lt. Co. B, Nov. 11, 1862.

Waterman, George F. Promoted from Pvt. Co. K, Jan. 13, 1863. WIA May 3, 1863 near Suffolk, VA. Promoted to 1st Lt. Co. C, Sept. 15, 1863.

West, Walter E. Promoted from Sgt. Co. C, Oct. 1, 1861. Promoted to 1st Lt. Co. C, Aug. 11, 1862. On staff duty and never served with company.

First Sergeants

Costello, George B. Promoted from Sgt. April 11, 1864. WIA, shot in right arm, July 30, 1864 at the Crater, Petersburg, VA. Promoted to 2nd Lt. Co. B, July 30, 1864.

Munroe, Charles W. Residence, East Greenwich. Enlisted Sept. 5, 1862. Promoted to 2nd Lt. Co. G, Oct. 11, 1861.

Farley, James H. Promoted from Sgt. Oct. 11, 1861. WIA, shot in hip, Sept. 17, 1862 at Antietam, MD. Promoted to 2nd Lt. Co. C, April 11, 1864.

Sergeants

Costello, George B. Promoted from Corp. Jan. 13, 1863. Promoted to 1st Sgt. April 11, 1864.

Croning, Dennis. Promoted from Corp. WIA, shot in side, July 30, 1864 at the Crater, Petersburg, VA. Trans. to Co. D, 7th R.I. Vols. Oct. 21, 1864. Mustered out July 13, 1865.

Farley, James H. Residence, Scituate. 32. S. Machinist. Enlisted Sept. 9, 1861. Promoted to 1st Sgt. Oct. 11, 1861.

Kibby, George L. Residence, Providence. 20. M. Courier. Enlisted Sept. 9, 1861. Promoted to Sgt. Maj. Jan. 13, 1863.

Martin, William H. Residence, Providence. 21. S. Book binder. Enlisted Sept. 9, 1861. WIA, shot in shoulder, Sept. 17, 1862 at Antietam, MD. Discharged for disability Dec. 31, 1862 at Washington, DC. Interred at Grace Church Cemetery, Providence, RI.

Morris, John F. Promoted from Corp. Nov. 13, 1861. Mustered out Oct. 15, 1864. Died 1907. Interred at North Burial Ground, Providence, RI.

Phillips, William A. Residence, Johnston. M. 32. Millwright. Enlisted Sept. 9, 1861. Promoted to Sgt. Maj. Oct. 7, 1863.

Corporals

Burlingame, Benjamin W. Promoted from Pvt. Dec. 1862. WIA, shot in hand, Dec. 13, 1862 at Fredericksburg, VA. Trans. to Co. B, 7th R.I. Vols. Oct. 21, 1864. Mustered out June 9, 1865. Died April 25, 1896. Interred at Knotty Oak Cemetery, Coventry, RI.

Crandall, George W. Promoted from Pvt. Nov. 13, 1861. WIA Mar. 14, 1862 at New Bern, NC. Trans. to VRC July 1, 1863. Died Jan. 17, 1885. Interred at White Brook Cemetery, Richmond, RI.

Croning, Dennis. Promoted from Pvt. Feb. 1, 1863. Promoted to Sgt.

Costello, George B. Promoted from Pvt. Nov. 13, 1861. Promoted to Sgt. Jan. 13, 1863.

Douglas, George L. Promoted from Pvt. Trans. to Co. D, 7th R.I. Vols. Oct. 21, 1864. Mustered out July 13, 1865. Died 1921. Interred at Hopkins Mill Cemetery, Foster, RI.

Dyer, Byron W. Promoted from Pvt. KIA July 30, 1864 at the Crater, Petersburg, VA.

Gibson, Nelson W. Residence, Johnston. 23. S. Machinist. Enlisted Sept. 5, 1861. Deserted in the face of the enemy Sept. 17, 1862 at Antietam, MD.

Greene, Charles H. Residence, Providence. 36. M. Engineer. Enlisted Sept. 24, 1861. Mustered out Oct. 15, 1864. Died July 22, 1901. Interred at North Burial Ground, Providence, RI.

Greene, Thomas L. Residence, Providence. 18. S. Laborer. Enlisted Sept. 5, 1861. Deserted Aug. 1862 near Fredericksburg, VA. Died Feb. 12, 1900. Interred at Glenford Cemetery, Scituate, RI.

Harrington, William E. Promoted from Pvt. Trans. to Co. D, 7th R.I. Vols. Oct. 21, 1864. Mustered out July 13, 1865.

Hill, Jerry. Promoted from Pvt. WIA, shot in shoulder, Sept. 17, 1862 at Antietam, MD. Trans. to Co. D, 7th R.I. Vols. Oct. 21, 1864. Mustered out July 13, 1865.

Kendall, John. Promoted from Pvt. Jan. 1, 1863. WIA, shot in left arm, July 30, 1864 at the Crater, Petersburg, VA. Mustered out Oct. 15, 1864. Died April 20, 1911. Interred at North Burial Ground, Providence, RI.

Lawrence, George P. Residence, Providence. 23. M. Operative. Enlisted Sept. 9, 1861. WIA, Mar. 14, 1862 at New Bern, NC. Discharged for disability Mar. 27, 1863.

Monroe, Charles W. Residence, East Greenwich. 31. S. Clerk. Promoted to 2nd Lt. Co. G, Oct. 11, 1862.

Morris, John F. 21. S. Residence, Johnston. Moulder. Enlisted Sept. 9, 1861. Promoted to Sgt. Nov. 13, 1861.

Nolan, Michael. Residence, Newport. 36. M. Laborer. Enlisted Sept. 9, 1861. Discharged for disability Oct. 10, 1862 at Sharpsburg, MD. Died Jan. 14, 1891. Interred at St. Mary's Cemetery, Newport, RI.

Musician

Cooke, Albert H. Residence, Taunton, MA. 17. S. Farmer. Enlisted Sept. 23, 1861. Trans. to VRC July 15, 1863.

Wagoner

Andrews, Israel. Residence, Coventry. Enlisted Sept. 9, 1861. Mustered out Oct. 15, 1864. Died Nov. 23, 1909. Interred at Pine Grove Cemetery, Coventry, RI.

Privates

Anness, Jesse L. Residence, Providence. 19. S. Butcher. Enlisted Sept. 5, 1861. Trans. to Co. B, 7th R.I. Vols. Oct. 21, 1864. Mustered out July 13, 1865. Died July 11, 1870. Interred at North Burial Ground, Providence, RI.

Arnold, John H. Residence, Woonsocket. 20. S. Clerk. Enlisted June 10, 1862. CIA July 30, 1864 at the Crater, Petersburg, VA. Mustered out Feb. 22, 1865.

Babcock, George W. Residence, South Kingstown. 21. S. Sailor. Enlisted Sept. 11, 1861. Deserted July 30, 1862 near Newport News, VA. Died June 18, 1894. Interred at Oak Grove Cemetery, New Bedford, MA.

Bicknell, Beriah. Residence, Johnston. 25. M. Carder. Enlisted Sept. 9, 1861. Discharged for disability Aug. 19, 1862 at Fredericksburg, VA. Died Sept. 29, 1912. Interred at Haven Hill Cemetery, Olney, IL.

Bills, Samuel D. Residence, Providence. Enlisted April 11, 1864. Died of typhoid Aug. 6, 1864 at Washington, DC. Interred at Arlington National Cemetery, Arlington, VA. Section 13, Grave 7726.

Briggs, Edward C. Residence, Somerset, MA. 18. S. Farmer. Enlisted Sept. 9, 1861. Trans. to Co. D, 7th R.I. Vols. Oct. 21, 1864. Mustered out July 13, 1865.

Briggs, Nathan. Residence, Coventry. 35. M. Laborer. Enlisted Aug. 5, 1862. Trans. to Co. D, 7th R.I. Vols. Oct. 21, 1864. Mustered out June 9, 1865. Died Sept. 17, 1894. Interred at Knotty Oak Cemetery, Coventry, RI.

Burlingame, Benjamin W. Residence, Warwick. Enlisted Aug. 7, 1862. WIA, shot in chest, Sept. 17, 1862 at Antietam, MD. Promoted to Corp. Dec. 1862.

Cameron, David H. Residence, Coventry. 23. M. Operative. Enlisted Sept. 11, 1861. MWIA Mar. 14, 1862 at New Bern, NC. DOW April 6, 1862 at New Bern, NC. Interred at New Bern National Cemetery, New Bern, NC. Section 11, Grave 1865.

Capwell, Jabez W. Residence, Warwick. 34. M. Operative. Enlisted Sept. 9, 1861. Discharged for disability Feb. 25, 1863 at Washington, DC. Died April 13, 1887. Interred at Greenwood Cemetery, Warwick, RI.

Chapman, Henry. Residence, Providence. 19. S. Farmer. Enlisted Sept. 9, 1861. Died of pneumonia Jan. 15, 1862 at Annapolis, MD.

Chappell, George W. Residence, Warwick. 38. M. Mechanic. Enlisted Sept. 10, 1861. Discharged for disability Nov. 3, 1862 at Providence, RI. Interred at Mineral Spring Cemetery, Pawtucket,

RI.

Cherry, James. Residence, Providence. 18. S. Laborer. Enlisted Sept. 9, 1861. Deserted in the face of the enemy Sept. 17, 1862 at Antietam, MD.

Clarke, Thomas. Residence, Providence. 34. M. Operative. Enlisted Sept. 6, 1861. Sent to Portsmouth Grove Hospital Sept. 2, 1862. Deserted Nov. 8, 1862. Interred at Pocasset Cemetery, Cranston, RI.

Cooke, Henry N. Residence, Warwick. 18. S. Farmer. Enlisted Sept. 9, 1861. Discharged for disability Dec. 14, 1861 at Camp California, VA.

Cooney, Michael J. Residence, Providence. 19. S. Machinist. Enlisted Sept. 9, 1861. Deserted in the face of the enemy Sept. 17, 1862 at Antietam, MD. Interred at St. Ann's Cemetery, Cranston, RI.

Costello, George B. Residence, Providence. 21. S. File cutter. Enlisted Sept. 11, 1861. Promoted to Corp. Nov. 13, 1861.

Crandall, George W. Residence, Charlestown. 25. M. Carder. Enlisted Sept. 9, 1861. Promoted to Corp. Nov. 13, 1861.

Croning, Dennis. Residence, Providence. 21. S. Machinist. Enlisted Sept. 11, 1861. Promoted to Corp. Feb. 1, 1863.

Curtis, John W. Residence, North Bridgewater, MA. 26. S. Farmer. Enlisted Aug. 15, 1862. Trans. to Co. A, 5th R.I. Heavy Artillery. Oct. 25, 1863. Died Mar. 29, 1906. Interred at Mt. Vernon Cemetery, Abington, MA.

Dailey, Daniel. Residence, Providence. 21. S. Sailor. Enlisted Sept. 11, 1861. Died of typhoid Aug. 18, 1862 at Roanoke, NC.

Donahue, John. Residence, Providence. 23. S. Spindle Maker. Enlisted Sept. 9, 1861. Discharged for disability Jan. 30, 1863 at Alexandria, VA.

Douglas, George L. Residence, Scituate. 21. S. Operative. Enlisted Sept. 9, 1861. Promoted to Corp.

Dow, Byron E. Residence, Providence. 21. S. Machinist. Enlisted Sept. 9, 1861. Trans. to Co. D, 7th R.I. Vols. Oct. 21, 1864. Mustered out July 13, 1865. Died June 16, 1869 "of disease contracted in the U.S. service during the Great Rebellion." Interred at Locust Grove Cemetery, Providence, RI.

Drinkwater, David G. Residence, Portland, ME. 22. S. Clerk. Enlisted Dec. 19, 1862. Deserted near Falmouth, VA, Jan. 6, 1863. Died Sept. 24, 1897. Interred at Evergreen Cemetery, Portland, ME.

Dyer, Byron. Residence, Cranston. 21. S. Farmer. Enlisted Aug. 17, 1862. Promoted to Corp.

Everett, William H. Residence, Providence. 18. S. Book Keeper. Enlisted Sept. 9, 1861. Mustered out Oct. 15, 1864. Died June 30, 1868. Interred at Swan Point Cemetery, Providence, RI.

Fish, Samuel C. Residence, Providence. 26. S. Jeweler. Enlisted Sept. 24, 1861. Mustered out Oct. 15, 1864. Died April 8, 1911. Interred at Oakland Cemetery, Cranston, RI.

Flanigan, Jeremiah. Residence, Taunton, MA. 23. S. Teamster. Enlisted Nov. 3, 1862. Deserted June 19, 1863 at Portsmouth, VA.

Fletcher, William H. Residence, Pawtucket. 21. M. Mechanic. Enlisted Sept. 9, 1861. Mustered out Oct. 15, 1864.

Forrest, James M, Residence, Attleboro, MA. 39. M. Moulder. Enlisted Sept. 9, 1861. Discharged for disability Feb. 19, 1863 at Washington, DC. Died Jan. 17, 1880. Interred at Togus National Cemetery, Augusta, ME. Grave 235.

Franklin, George W. Residence, Scituate. 30. M. Operative. Enlisted Sept. 9, 1861. Discharged for disability May 1, 1862 at Beaufort, NC. Died Dec. 29, 1907. Interred at New Westfield Cemetery, Danielson, CT.

Gardiner, Andrew J. Residence, Warwick. 32. M. Operative. Enlisted Sept. 9, 1861. Trans to VRC July 15, 1864.

Greenman, Henry C. Residence, Providence. 28. M. Operative. Enlisted Sept. 5, 1861. Deserted in the face of the enemy Sept. 17, 1862 at Antietam, MD.

Gorton, Henry W. Residence, Coventry. 19. S. Farmer. Died of tuberculosis Dec. 14, 1862 at Falmouth, VA. Interred at Gorton Lot, Coventry Cemetery 83, Coventry, RI.

Hanley, James. Residence, Smithfield. 32. S. Operative. Enlisted Sept. 12, 1862. Trans. to Co. D, 7th R.I. Vols. Oct. 21, 1864.

Hanley, Thomas. Residence, Providence. 25. S. Operative. Enlisted Dec. 2, 1862. CIA July 30, 1864 at the Crater, Petersburg, VA. Trans. to Co. D, 7th R.I. Vols. Oct. 21, 1864. Mustered out July 13, 1865. Interred at St. Francis Cemetery, Pawtucket, RI.

Hardman, Robert. Residence, Newport. 21. S. Farmer. Enlisted Aug. 15, 1862. Died of typhoid Feb. 24, 1863 at Washington, DC. Interred at Island Cemetery, Newport, RI.

Harrington, William E. Residence, Providence. 18. S. Butcher. Enlisted Sept. 9, 1861. Promoted to Corp.

Harris, Jabez L. Residence, Rehoboth, MA. 23. S. Farmer. Enlisted Sept. 9, 1861. Discharged for disability Feb. 25, 1863 at Washington, DC. Died Dec. 1, 1900. Interred at Pocasset Cemetery, Cranston, RI.

Hendrick, Benjamin W. Residence, Providence. 28. S. Jeweler. Enlisted Sept. 9, 1861. Discharged for disability Jan. 2, 1863 at

Providence, RI. Died of disease contracted in the service at Rehoboth, MA, Mar. 25, 1866. Interred at Jonathan Wheeler Cemetery, Rehoboth, MA.

Hersey, Simeon. Residence, Providence. 18. S. Operative. Enlisted Sept. 9, 1861. Deserted Sept. 5, 1862 at Washington, DC.

Hill, Albert H. Residence, Scituate. 21. S. Operative. Enlisted July 1, 1862. Trans. to Co. D, 7th R.I. Vols. Oct. 21, 1864. Mustered out June 9, 1865. Died Sept. 24, 1901. Interred at Union Cemetery, Moosup, CT.

Hill, Jerry. Residence, Scituate. 24. M. Operative. Enlisted Sept. 9, 1861. Promoted to Corp.

Hill, Joseph. Residence, Scituate. 21. S. Farmer. Enlisted Sept. 9, 1861. Trans. to Co. D, 7th R.I. Vols. Oct. 21, 1864. Mustered out June 9, 1865. Died 1894. Interred at Riverside Cemetery, Hiram Rapids, OH.

Holden, Joseph K. Residence, Charlestown. 17. S. Clerk. Enlisted Sept. 9, 1861. Discharged for disability Nov. 22, 1862 at Alexandria, VA. Died 1927. Interred at Pocasset Cemetery, Cranston, RI.

Holmes, Daniel. Residence, Providence. 18. S. Machinist. Enlisted Sept. 27, 1861. Mustered out Oct. 15, 1864. Died 1928. Interred at North Burial Ground, Providence, RI.

Horton, Charles. Residence, Providence. 39. S. Farmer. Enlisted Sept. 10, 1861. Discharged for disability May 1, 1862 at Beaufort, NC. Interred at Lakeside-Carpenter Cemetery, East Providence, RI.

Hunt, Leonard A. Residence, Coventry. 18. S. Farmer. Enlisted April 11, 1864. Trans. to Co. D. 7th R.I. Vols. Oct. 21, 1864.

Johnson, Daniel. Residence, East Greenwich. 42. S. Laborer. Enlisted Sept. 9, 1851. Mustered out Oct. 15, 1864. Died July 23,

1888. Interred at Capt. Allen Johnson Lot, East Greenwich Cemetery 30, East Greenwich, RI.

Kendall, John. Residence, Providence. 21. S. Jeweler. Enlisted Sept. 9, 1861. Promoted to Corp. Jan. 1, 1863.

Kettle, Charles A. Residence, Westerly. 33. M. Spinner. Enlisted Aug. 5,1862. Trans to Co. D, 7th R.I. Vols. Oct. 21, 1864. Mustered out June 9, 1865,

Knowles, Truman M. Residence, Smithfield. 43. M. Farmer. Enlisted Sept. 9, 1861. Mustered out Oct. 21, 1864.

Larvee, William L. Residence, Cranston. 18. S. Farmer. Enlisted Sept. 9, 1861. Mustered out Oct. 15, 1864.

Luther, John F. Residence, Providence. 19. S. Spindle maker. Enlisted Sept. 9, 1861. Mustered out Oct. 15, 1864.

Lynch, Daniel. Residence, Providence. 30. M. Laborer. Enlisted Sept. 10, 1861. WIA, shot in shoulder, Sept. 17, 1862 at Antietam, MD. Trans. to Co. D, 7th R.I. Vols. Oct. 21, 1864. Mustered out July 13, 1865. Died Jan. 11, 1873. Interred at St. Patrick's Cemetery, Providence, RI.

McCann, James. Residence, Smithfield. 42. M. Operative. Enlisted Nov. 1, 1862. WIA, shot in knee, July 30, 1864 at the Crater, Petersburg, VA. Trans. to Co. D, 7th R.I. Vols. Oct. 21, 1864. Mustered out July 13, 1865.

McCormick, Daniel. Residence, Providence. 47. M. Mechanic. Discharged for disability Oct. 25, 1862 at Washington, DC.

McGowen, William. Residence, Providence. 18. S. Mechanic. Enlisted Sept. 9, 1861. KIA Sept. 17, 1862 at Antietam, MD. Interred at Antietam National Cemetery, Sharpsburg, MD. Rhode Island Section, Grave 2831.

McHugh, Peter. Residence, Providence. 18. S. Sailor. Enlisted April 4, 1864. Trans. to Co. D, 7th R.I. Vols. Oct. 21, 1864. Mustered out July 13, 1865. Died Mar. 25, 1897. Interred at St. Francis Cemetery, Pawtucket, RI.

McKinley, Thomas. Residence, Cumberland. 23. S. Sailor. Enlisted Jan. 12, 1863. Deserted May 30, 1864 near Portsmouth, VA.

McMahon, Patrick. Residence, Providence. 18. S. Dyer. Enlisted Sept. 9, 1861. Trans. to U.S. Navy Oct. 24, 1862. Interred at St. Francis Cemetery, Pawtucket, RI.

McNamee, Miles M. Residence, Providence. 26. M. Machinist. Enlisted Oct. 27, 1861. Died of typhoid Jan. 1, 1863 at Washington, DC.

McQuernan, Terrance. Residence, Providence. 20. S. Laborer. Enlisted Mar. 9, 1864. Trans. to Co. D, 7th R.I. Vols. Oct. 21, 1864.

Martin, George. Residence, Johnston. 15. S. Operative. Enlisted Sept. 10, 1861. KIA July 24, 1864 at Petersburg, VA. Interred at City Point National Cemetery, Hopewell, VA. Grave 2663.

Martin, James. Residence, Johnston. 18. S. Operative. Enlisted Sept. 10, 1861. Mustered out Oct. 15, 1864. Interred at Union Village Cemetery, North Smithfield, RI.

Miller, William A. Residence, Bristol. 18. S. Laborer. Enlisted Sept. 12, 1861. Died of dysentery Mar. 30, 1862 at Roanoke, NC. Interred at North Burial Ground, Bristol, RI.

Miller, William H. Residence, Rehoboth, MA. 22. M. Farmer. Enlisted Sept. 9, 1861. Deserted in the face of the enemy Sept. 17, 1862 at Antietam, MD.

Moody, John. Residence, Providence. 31. M. Farmer. Enlisted Sept. 10, 1861. Trans. to Co. D, 7th R.I. Vols. Oct. 21, 1864.

Moon, Oliver. Residence, Coventry. 34. M. Farmer. Enlisted Aug. 2, 1862. WIA, shot in back, Sept. 17, 1862 at Antietam, MD. Trans. to Co. D, 7th R.I. Vols. Oct. 21, 1864. Mustered out June 9, 1865. Interred at Knotty Oak Cemetery, Coventry, RI.

Morrison, John. Residence, Providence. 21. S. Laborer. Enlisted June 26, 1862. Deserted Sept. 4, 1862 near Frederick, MD. Died Feb. 18, 1913. Interred at Moshassuck Cemetery, Central Falls, RI.

Murphy, John. Residence, Providence. 21. Enlisted Sept. 9, 1861. Died of typhoid at Roanoke, NC, Feb. 20, 1862. Interred at New Bern National Cemetery, New Bern, NC. Section 11, Grave 1911.

O'Dell, Elijah W. Residence, New York, NY. 18. S. Laborer. Enlisted Sept. 10, 1861. Deserted at Newport News, VA, July 1, 1862.

O'Dell, George W. Residence, New York, NY. 21. S. Teamster. Enlisted Sept. 10, 1861. Trans. to Co. D, 7th R.I. Vols. Oct. 21, 1864. Transferred to VRC in 1865.

Olsen, Henry. Residence, New York, NY. 20. S. Farmer. Enlisted Jan. 22, 1863. Trans. to Co. D, 7th R.I. Vols. Oct. 21, 1864. Mustered out July 13, 1865.

Ormsbee, William W. Residence, Richmond. 19. S. Laborer. Enlisted Sept. 9, 1861. Trans. to Co. B, 7th R.I. Vols. Oct. 21, 1864. Mustered out July 13, 1865. Died June 26, 1917. Interred at Black Point Cemetery, Scarborough, ME.

Pitts, George. Residence, Providence. 22. M. Carpenter. Enlisted Aug. 15, 1862. Trans. to Co. D, 7th R.I. Vols. Oct. 21, 1864. Mustered out June 9, 1865. Died Mar. 4, 1906. Interred at Locust Grove Cemetery, Providence, RI.

Pitts, Joseph. Residence, Providence. Enlisted Aug. 15, 1862. Trans. to Co. D, 7th R.I. Vols. Oct. 21, 1864. Died Dec. 10, 1913. Interred at Unitarian Church Cemetery, Dighton, MA.

Potter, George. Residence, Coventry. 18. S. Farmer. Enlisted Sept. 10, 1862. Discharged for disability Nov. 21, 1862 at Baltimore, MD.

Potter, Thomas. Residence, Coventry. 21. S. Farmer. Enlisted Sept. 10, 1861. Deserted at Fredericksburg, VA, Aug. 1, 1862.

Powers, James. Residence, Providence. 18. S. Chair maker. Enlisted Sept. 9, 1861. Deserted July 1, 1862 at Newport News, VA.

Prestwick, Thomas. Residence, Providence. 17. S. Jeweler. Enlisted Sept. 9, 1861. Trans. to Co. D, 7th R.I. Vols. Oct. 21, 1864. Mustered out July 13, 1865.

Rigley, Thomas. Residence, North Providence. 23. M. Seaman. Enlisted Sept. 10, 1861. Deserted Sept. 4, 1862 near Washington, DC.

Ross, John. Residence, Providence. 32. S. Sailor. Enlisted Jan. 7, 1863. Deserted Mar. 27, 1863 near Newport News, VA.

Sheridan, Patrick. Residence, Providence. 23. M. Painter. Enlisted Sept. 9, 1861. KIA Mar. 14, 1862 at New Bern, NC.

Shore, George A. Residence, Swansea, MA. 28. S. Machinist. Enlisted Sept. 9, 1862. Trans. to VRC Aug. 6, 1864.

Smith, Thomas E. Residence, Newburyport, MA. 19. S. Sailor. Enlisted Mar. 14, 1864. KIA July 30, 1864 at the Crater, Petersburg, VA.

Stacey, Michael E. Residence, Providence. 19. S. Laborer. Enlisted Aug. 7, 1862. KIA Sept. 17, 1862 at Antietam, MD.

Interred at Antietam National Cemetery, Sharpsburg, MD. Rhode Island Section, Grave 2826.

Sullivan, Michael. Residence, Providence. 18. S. Bootmaker. Enlisted Sept. 9, 1861. Trans. to U.S. Navy Oct. 24, 1862.

Tanner, Thomas D. Residence, Providence. 18. S. Farmer. Enlisted Sept. 11, 1861. Trans. to VRC Aug. 1, 1863.

Tiernan, John B. Residence, Boston, MA. 19. S. Bootmaker. Enlisted July 27, 1864. Trans. to Co. D, 7th R.I. Vols. Oct. 21, 1864. Mustered out July 13, 1865. Died Aug. 4, 1918. Interred at Granger Fairview Cemetery, Granger, OH.

Tillinghast, Henry M. Residence, East Greenwich. 20. S. Farmer. Enlisted Sept. 9, 1861. Promoted to 2nd Lt. Dec. 12, 1862 and transferred to Co. D, 12th R.I. Vols. Died June 4, 1915. Interred at Job Tillinghast Lot, East Greenwich Cemetery 32, East Greenwich, RI.

Tillinghast, William W. Residence, East Greenwich. 35. M. Farmer. Enlisted Sept. 9, 1861. WIA Mar. 14, 1862 at New Bern, NC. Discharged for disability Oct. 29, 1862 at Providence, RI. "Died of war wounds" Aug. 27, 1866 at East Greenwich, RI. Interred at Elm Grove Cemetery, North Kingstown, RI.

Travers, Thomas. Residence, Richmond. 24. M. Farmer. Enlisted Mar. 23, 1864. WIA, shot in right arm, July 30, 1864 at the Crater, Petersburg, VA. Trans. to Co. D, 7th R.I. Vols. Oct. 21, 1864. Mustered out July 13, 1865.

Tripp, Alden. Residence, Tiverton. 32. M. Farmer. Enlisted April 1, 1864. KIA July 30, 1864 at the Crater, Petersburg, VA.

Vallett, Leander N. Residence, Providence. 22. M. Clerk. Enlisted Sept. 9, 1861. Mustered out Oct. 15, 1864. Died 1926. Interred at Pocasset Cemetery, Cranston, RI.

Viall, William S. Residence, Rehoboth, MA. 22. S. Farmer. Enlisted Sept. 11, 1861. Trans. to Co. D, 7th R.I. Vols. Oct. 21, 1864. Mustered out July 13, 1865. Died Sept. 12, 1890. Interred at Harrington Cemetery, Cuyahoga Falls, OH.

Wood, Caleb G. Residence, Coventry. 22. M. Laborer. Enlisted Aug. 4, 1862. Trans to Co. D, 7th R.I. Vols. Oct. 21, 1864. Mustered out June 9, 1865. Died Nov. 30, 1911. Interred at Large Maple Root Cemetery, Coventry, RI.

Webb, William S. Residence, Providence. 18. S. Farmer. Enlisted Sept. 9, 1861. Deserted Sept. 4, 1862 near Washington, DC.

Woodward, Gideon P. Residence, North Stonington, CT. 36. M. Mason. Enlisted June 20, 1862. Discharged for disability Oct. 17, 1862 at New York, NY.

COMPANY D

Captains

Kenyon, Nelson. Residence, Coventry. 45. M. Merchant. Commissioned Oct. 2, 1861. Resigned Aug. 11, 1862. Died June 2, 1898. Interred at North Burial Ground, Bristol, RI.

Read, Walter A. Promoted from 1st Lt. Co. D, Aug. 11, 1862. In command of the regiment Aug. 1, 1864 to Oct. 15, 1864. Mustered out Oct. 15,1864. Died 1918. Interred at Acotes Hill Cemetery, Glocester, RI.

First Lieutenants

Jenckes, Allen. Promoted from 2nd Lt. Co. D, Aug. 13, 1863. Mustered out Oct. 15, 1864. Died July 10, 1907. Interred at Oak Hill Cemetery, Providence, RI.

Read, Walter A. Promoted from 2nd Lt. Co. D, Nov. 20, 1861. Promoted to Capt. Co. D, Aug. 11, 1862.

Watts, George H. Promoted from 2nd Lt. Co. D, Nov. 1, 1862. Resigned Aug. 13, 1863.

Second Lieutenants

Baker, Otis A. Promoted from 1st Sgt. Co. A, Nov. 20, 1861. Resigned Aug. 11, 1862. Died June 14, 1910. Interred at Village Cemetery, Rehoboth, MA.

Buffum, George R. Promoted from Sgt. Aug. 11, 1862. MWIA, shot in chest, Sept. 17, 1862 at Antietam, MD. DOW Oct. 21,

1862 at Sharpsburg, MD. Interred at Antietam National Cemetery, Sharpsburg, MD. Officer's Section.

Jenckes, Allen. Promoted from Sgt. Co. E, Jan. 13, 1863. Promoted to 1st Lt. Co. D, Aug. 13, 1863.

Kibby, George L. Promoted from Sgt. Maj. Sept. 26, 1863. CIA July 30, 1864 at the Crater, Petersburg, VA. Mustered out Oct. 15, 1864. Died Feb. 21, 1909. Interred at Walpole Village Cemetery, Walpole, NH.

Read, Walter A. Residence, Glocester. 21. M. Clerk. Commissioned Sept. 30, 1861. Promoted to 1st Lt. Co. D, Nov. 20, 1861.

Watts, George H. Promoted from Sgt. Co. D, Oct. 21, 1862. Promoted to 1st Lt. Co. D, Nov. 1, 1862.

First Sergeants

Andrews, Dennis P. Residence, Burrillville. 29. M. Clerk. Enlisted Sept. 25, 1861. Promoted to 2nd Lt. Co. H, May 4, 1862.

Guild, Charles E. Promoted from Sgt. May 4, 1862. MWIA Sept. 17, 1862 at Antietam, MD. DOW Sept. 25, 1862 at Sharpsburg, MD. Interred at Acotes Hill Cemetery, Glocester, RI.

Lamson, George F. Promoted from Sgt. Nov. 1, 1862. Mustered out Oct. 15, 1864. Died 1913. Interred at Pascoag Cemetery, Burrillville, RI.

Sergeants

Buffum, George R. Promoted from Corp. Nov. 20, 1861. Promoted to 2nd Lt. Co. D, Aug. 11, 1862.

Campbell, George. Promoted from Corp. Jan. 1863. Mustered out Oct. 15, 1864.

Carpenter, George B. Promoted from Corp. Nov. 1, 1862. WIA, right arm amputated, July 30, 1864 at the Crater, Petersburg, VA. Mustered out Oct. 15, 1864. Died May 23, 1914. Interred at First Cemetery, Hopkinton, RI.

Caswell, William H. Promoted from Corp. June 15, 1862. Discharged for disability Dec. 31, 1862 at Alexandria, VA. Died May 20, 1889. Interred at Greenwood Cemetery, Coventry, RI.

Guild, Charles E. Residence, Glocester. 21. S. Carpenter. Enlisted Sept. 9, 1861. Promoted to 1st Sgt. May 4, 1862.

Hill, Charles F. Promoted from Corp. Aug. 15, 1862. Mustered out Oct. 15, 1864. Died Sept. 19, 1897. Interred at Oak Grove Cemetery, Fall River, MA.

Lamson, George F. Promoted from Pvt. Nov. 13, 1861. Promoted to 1st Sgt. Nov. 1, 1862.

Lawton, John D. Promoted from Pvt. Nov. 13, 1861. Mustered out Oct. 15, 1864. Died June 30, 1918. Interred at New Scotland Cemetery, Scotland, CT.

Mowry, Emor W. Promoted from Corp. Nov. 11, 1862. Mustered out Oct. 15, 1864. Died 1919. Interred at Harrisville Cemetery, Burrillville, RI.

Starkweather, Henry. Residence, Glocester. 24. S. Clerk. Promoted to 2nd Lt. Co. K, Nov. 20, 1862.

Watts, George H. Residence, Burrillville. 30. M. Operative. Enlisted Sept. 9, 1861. WIA Sept. 17, 1862 at Antietam, MD. Promoted to 2nd Lt. Co. D, Oct. 21, 1862.

Corporals

Buffum, George R. Residence, Burrillville. 19. S. Laborer. Enlisted Aug. 8, 1861. Promoted to Sgt. Nov. 20, 1861.

Burdick, Benjamin F. Promoted from Pvt. KIA Sept. 17, 1862 at Antietam, MD. Interred at Antietam National Cemetery, Sharpsburg, MD. Rhode Island Section, Grave 2928. Cenotaph at Rockville Cemetery, Hopkinton, RI.

Campbell, George. Promoted from Pvt. Mar. 14, 1862. Promoted to Sgt. Jan. 1863.

Carpenter, George B. Promoted from Pvt. June 20, 1862. Promoted to Sgt. Nov. 1, 1862.

Caswell, William H. Residence, Burrillville. 29. S. Laborer. Enlisted Sept. 29, 1861. Promoted to Sgt. June 15, 1862.

Gates, William H. Promoted from Pvt. Nov. 1, 1862. Mustered out Oct. 15, 1864. Interred at Moshassuck Cemetery, Central Falls, RI.

Harris, Andrew F. Residence, Burrillville. 39. M. Gentleman. Enlisted Sept. 25, 1861. Discharged for disability Oct. 6, 1862 at Washington, DC. Died in Nov. 3, 1863 of disease contracted in the service at Burrillville, RI. Interred at Acotes Hill Cemetery, Glocester, RI.

Hill, Charles F. Promoted from Pvt. Nov. 13, 1861. Promoted to Sgt. Aug. 15, 1862.

Johnson, Richard M. Promoted from Pvt. Aug. 15, 1862. Mustered out Oct. 15, 1864. Died 1927. Interred at Knotty Oak Cemetery, Coventry, RI.

Mowry, Emor W. Residence, Burrillville.23. S. Mason. Enlisted Sept. 9, 1861. WIA, shot in back, Sept. 17, 1862 at Antietam, MD. Promoted to Sgt. Nov. 11, 1862.

Oakley, John. Promoted from Pvt. WIA, shot in arm, July 30, 1864 at the Crater, Petersburg, VA. Mustered out Oct. 15, 1864. Interred at Island Cemetery, Newport, RI. Interred at Island Cemetery, Newport, RI.

Shay, John. Promoted from Pvt. Sept. 25, 1862. Mustered out Oct. 15, 1864.

Smith, Seneca N. Promoted from Pvt. Sept. 25, 1862. Mustered out Oct. 15, 1864. Died April 13, 1895. Interred at Duty Smith Lot, Burrillville Cemetery 21, Burrillville, RI.

Starkweather, Marshall H. Residence, Glocester. 21. S. Laborer. Enlisted Sept. 9, 1861. Discharged for disability Dec. 31, 1863 near Portsmouth, VA. Died Jan. 31, 1919. Interred at High Street Cemetery, Killingly, CT.

Sweet, Henry C. Promoted from Pvt. Nov. 13, 1862. Discharged for disability Dec. 15, 1862 at Alexandria, VA. Died Mar. 16, 1875. Interred at Dr. Nathaniel Sweet Lot, Glocester Cemetery 13, Glocester, RI.

Thayer, Henry R. Residence, Burrillville. 27. S. Farmer. Died of typhoid Jan. 2, 1862 at Washington, DC. Interred at Pascoag Cemetery, Burrillville, RI.

Musician

Daggett, Joel M. Residence, Glocester. 46. M. Farmer. Enlisted Sept. 9, 1861. Mustered out Oct. 15, 1864. Interred at O'Brian Cemetery, Killingly, CT.

Wagoner

Kimball, Josiah. Residence, Burrillville. 20. S. Teamster. Enlisted Sept. 9, 1861. Trans. to Co. G, 7th R.I. Vols. Oct. 21, 1864. Mustered out July 13, 1865. Died Nov. 5, 1928. Interred at Mt. Vernon Cemetery, Mt. Vernon, Skagit County, Washington.

Privates

Adams, Henry. Residence, Glocester. 19. S. Shoemaker. Enlisted Aug. 10, 1861. Trans. to Regular Army, Oct. 24, 1862.

Albert, Richard W. Residence, Tiverton. 39. M. Seaman. Enlisted Aug. 24, 1861. Discharged for disability Feb. 20, 1863 at Newport News, VA. Died Mar. 15, 1907. Interred at Oak Grove Cemetery, Fall River, MA.

Andrews, James H. Residence, Glocester. 18. S. Laborer. Enlisted May 28, 1862. WIA, shot in leg, Dec. 13, 1862 at Fredericksburg, VA, Trans. to Co. G, 7th R.I. Vols. Oct. 21, 1864. Mustered out July 13, 1865. Died Mar. 9, 1885. Interred at Place-Keach Lot, Glocester Cemetery 25, Glocester, RI.

Angell, Sabin. Residence, Burrillville. 22. S. Laborer. Enlisted Sept. 9, 1861. Mustered out Oct. 15, 1864. Died 1900. Interred at Pine Grove Cemetery, Templeton, MA.

Arnold, Gilbert H. Residence, Burrillville. 21. M. Laborer. Enlisted Aug. 13, 1862. Mustered out Oct. 15, 1864. Mustered out June 9, 1865. Died Jan. 2, 1910. Interred at Union Cemetery, North Smithfield, RI.

Ballou, Charles F. Residence, Scituate. 31. S. Machinist. Enlisted Aug. 15, 1861. Discharged for disability Dec. 18, 1862 at Alexandria, VA. Died Mar. 8, 1913. Interred at Lovett Cemetery, Sprague, CT

Berry, Alfred B. Residence, Westerly. 18. S. Harness maker. Enlisted Sept. 27, 1861. Mustered out Oct. 15, 1864. Died Dec. 7, 1917. Interred at Oak Grove Cemetery, Hopkinton, RI.

Booth, Stephen. Residence, Smithfield. 21. S. Printer. Enlisted Sept. 19, 1861. Mustered out Oct. 15, 1864. Died Dec. 1, 1908. Interred at Forest Hills Cemetery, Boston, MA.

Bradley, Abraham. Residence, Burrillville. 22. S. Weaver. Enlisted Aug. 3, 1861. Trans to Co. G, 7th R.I. Vols. Oct. 21, 1864. Mustered out July 13, 1865. Died 1927. Interred at St. Patrick Cemetery, Hogansburg, NY.

Briggs, Nathan O. Residence, Glocester. 25. S. Shoemaker. Enlisted Sept. 16, 1862. Trans. to Co. G, 7th R.I. Vols. Oct. 21, 1864. Mustered out July 13, 1865. Died of tuberculosis contracted in the service June 6, 1867 at Putnam, CT. Interred at Grove Street Cemetery, Putnam, CT.

Burdick, Benjamin F. Residence, Hopkinton. 20. S. Farmer. Enlisted Sept. 27, 1861. Promoted to Corp.

Burlingame, Albert. Residence, Smithfield. 32. M. Farmer. Enlisted Sept. 4, 1861. Deserted Feb. 1, 1863 at Falmouth, VA. Died Mar. 25, 1876. Interred at Acotes Hill Cemetery, Glocester, RI.

Cahoone, Gideon A. Residence, Cranston. 21. S. Farmer. Enlisted Aug. 2, 1862. Trans. to Co. G, 7th R.I. Vols. Oct. 21, 1864. Mustered out June 9, 1865. Died July 28, 1912. Interred at Knotty Oak Cemetery, Coventry, RI.

Campbell, George. Residence, Burrillville. 33. S. Laborer. Enlisted Aug. 16, 1861. Promoted to Corp. Mar. 14. 1862.

Carpenter, George B. Residence, Westerly. M. 19. Student. Enlisted Sept. 23, 1861. Promoted to Corp. June 20, 1862.

Chamberlin, Edwin S. Residence, Burrillville. 35. M. Merchant. Enlisted Aug. 10, 1861. Discharged for disability Dec. 28, 1862 at Philadelphia, PA. Died April 5, 1874. Interred at Center Cemetery, Coventry, CT.

Chamberlin, Lewis. Residence, Burrillville. 35. M. Blacksmith. Enlisted Aug. 6, 1862. Discharged for disability Oct. 29, 1862. Died 1907. Interred at Center Cemetery, Coventry, CT.

Charles, Isaac. Residence, Smithfield. 19. S. Laborer. Enlisted Sept. 10, 1861. Mustered out Oct. 15, 1864. Died Jan. 26, 1919. Interred at Hillside Cemetery, Seabrook, NH.

Clarke, John T. Residence, Newport. 24. S. Blacksmith. Enlisted Aug. 27, 1861. KIA Mar. 14, 1862 at New Bern, NC. Interred at Common Burial Ground, Newport, RI.

Clemence, George B. Residence, Burrillville. 20. S. Laborer. Enlisted Sept. 9, 1861. WIA, shot in side, July 30, 1864 at the Crater, Petersburg, VA. Trans. to Co. G, 7th RI Vols. Oct. 21, 1864. Died 1926. Interred at Acotes Hill Cemetery, Glocester, RI.

Clemence, Moses. Residence, Smithfield. 22. S. Laborer. Enlisted Sept. 9, 1861. Mustered out Oct. 15, 1864. Died 1909. Interred at Oak Hill Cemetery, Woonsocket, RI.

Corey, John W. Residence, Warwick. 28. M. Laborer. Enlisted Sept. 14, 1861. Discharged for disability Sept. 25, 1863 at Portsmouth, VA. Died Mar. 17, 1902. Interred at Hunt-Hall Cemetery, North Kingstown Cemetery 11, North Kingstown, RI.

Crandall, Davis. Residence, Hopkinton. 21. S. Farmer. Enlisted Sept. 27, 1861. KIA Mar. 14, 1862 at New Bern, NC. Interred at Rockville Cemetery, Hopkinton, RI.

Crandall, William L. Residence, Westerly. 20. S. Farmer. Enlisted Sept. 25, 1861. Mustered out Oct. 15, 1864. Died Mar. 20, 1905. Interred at First Cemetery, Hopkinton, RI.

Cutting, Warren J. Residence, Smithfield. 22. M. Laborer. Enlisted Sept. 9, 1861. Deserted Aug. 15, 1862 near Fredericksburg, VA. Died 1922. Interred at Hope Cemetery, Worcester, MA.

Davis, James. Residence, Smithfield. 18. S. Laborer. Enlisted Sept. 11, 1861. KIA Aug. 19, 1864 at Hatcher's Run, VA. Interred at Poplar Spring National Cemetery, Petersburg, VA. Grave 1421.

Dorrance, Edward. Residence, Providence. 23. S. Trader. Enlisted Sept. 13, 1862. Discharged for disability April 30, 1863 at Washington, DC.

Francis, Samuel. Residence, Burrillville. 22. S. Farmer. Enlisted Sept. 23, 1861. Mustered out Oct. 15, 1864. Died Nov. 10, 1909. Interred at Togus National Cemetery, Augusta, ME. Grave 2622.

Friery, Felix. Residence, Burrillville. 38. M. Laborer. Enlisted Sept. 9, 1861. Mustered out Oct. 15, 1864. Died 1890. Interred at Pascoag Cemetery, Burrillville, RI.

Friery, Peter. Residence, Burrillville. 25. S. Farmer. Enlisted Sept. 9, 1861. CIA July 30, 1864 at the Crater, Petersburg, VA. Mustered out Dec. 1, 1864. Died 1906. Interred at Pascoag Cemetery, Burrillville, RI.

Gates, William H. Residence, Providence. 20. S. Jeweler. Enlisted Sept. 18, 1861. Promoted to Corp. Nov. 1, 1862.

Gavitt, Edwin D. Residence, Hopkinton. 18. S. Student. Enlisted Sept. 25, 1861. MWIA Mar. 14, 1862 at New Bern, NC. DOW June 16, 1862 at New York, NY. Interred at Oak Grove Cemetery, Hopkinton, RI.

Gleason, Daniel E. Residence, Glocester. 31. M. Farmer. Enlisted Oct. 1, 1861. Trans. to VRC Dec. 23, 1863. Died 1912. Interred at Acotes Hill Cemetery, Glocester, RI.

Gordon, Edward. Residence, Burrillville. 24. S. Weaver. Enlisted Sept. 9, 1861. Discharged for disability Jan. 29, 1863 at Alexandria, VA.

Hanley, James. Residence, Glocester. 22. M. Farmer. Enlisted Sept. 9, 1861. Mustered out Oct. 15, 1864. Died Oct. 25, 1926. Interred at St. Patrick's Cemetery, Burrillville, RI.

Hardy, John. Residence, Tiverton. 34. S. Laborer. Enlisted Sept. 17, 1861. KIA Sept. 17, 1862 at Antietam, MD. Interred at Antietam National Cemetery, Sharpsburg, MD. Rhode Island Section, Grave 2827.

Harris, Andrew F. Residence, Glocester. 18. S. Farmer. Enlisted Sept. 9, 1861. Died of typhoid Feb. 20, 1863 at Glocester, RI. Interred at Acotes Hill Cemetery, Glocester, RI.

Hawkins, Robert S. Residence, Scituate. 18. S. Farmer. Enlisted Sept. 9, 1861. Trans. to Co. G, 7th R.I. Vols. Oct. 21, 1864. Mustered out July 13, 1865. Died April 17, 1922. Interred at Pleasant View Cemetery, Barnet, VT.

Hill, Charles F. Residence, Tiverton. 26. M. Seaman. Enlisted Sept. 17, 1861. Promoted to Corp. Nov. 13, 1861.

Horton, Andrew J. Residence, Uxbridge, MA. 27. M. Shoemaker. Enlisted Sept. 23, 1861. Discharged for disability Dec. 28, 1862. Died Nov. 28, 1910. Interred at Oak Hill Cemetery, Woonsocket, RI.

Jenness, Nelson. Residence, Burrillville. 30. M. Farmer. MWIA July 30, 1864 at the Crater, Petersburg, VA. DOW Sept. 7, 1864 as a POW at Richmond, VA. Cenotaph at Hillcrest Cemetery, Hollis, ME.

Johnson, Richard M. Residence, Warwick. 20. M. Farmer. Enlisted Sept. 14, 1861. Promoted to Corp. Aug. 15, 1862.

Johnson, Stephen. Residence, Warwick. 21. S. Farmer. Enlisted Sept. 25, 1861. Mustered out Oct. 15, 1864. Died June 12, 1916. Interred at Union Cemetery, Plainfield, CT.

Lacey, James. Residence, Burrillville. 22. S. Laborer. Enlisted Sept. 9, 1861. Trans. to Co. G, 7th R.I. Vols. Oct. 21, 1864. Died Aug. 23, 1931. Interred at St. Patrick's Cemetery, Burrillville, RI.

Lamson, George F. Residence, Burrillville. 19. S. Laborer. Enlisted Sept. 9, 1861. Promoted to Sgt. Nov. 13, 1861.

Law, Jeremiah. Residence, Smithfield. 32. S. Farmer. Enlisted Sept. 28, 1861. Deserted Sept. 4, 1862 at Washington, DC. Died 1916. Interred at Slatersville Cemetery, North Smithfield, RI.

Lawton, John D. Residence, Hopkinton. 18. S. Operative. Enlisted Sept. 27, 1861. Promoted to Sgt. Nov. 13, 1861.

Lawrence, Orrin S. Residence, Glocester. 21. S. Teamster. Enlisted Sept. 9, 1861. WIA, shot in chest, Sept. 17, 1862 at Antietam, MD. Discharged for disability Sept. 3, 1863.

Leary, John. Residence, Warwick. 37. M. Seaman. Enlisted Sept. 9, 1861. Trans. to Co. G, 7th R.I. Vols. Oct. 21, 1864. Mustered out July 13, 1865.

Lockwood, Thomas H. Residence, Glocester. 37. M. Laborer. Enlisted Sept. 9, 1861. WIA Mar. 14, 1862 at New Bern, NC. Mustered out Oct. 15, 1864. Died 1906. Interred at Brayton Cemetery, Warwick, RI.

McCabe, Michael. Residence, Burrillville. 25. S. Laborer. Enlisted Sept. 9, 1861. KIA Sept. 17, 1862 at Antietam, MD.

McKee, Andrew. Residence, Warwick. 48. M. Operative. Enlisted July 17, 1862. Died in railroad accident Oct. 21, 1862 near Harpers Ferry, WV. Interred at North Burial Ground, Providence, RI.

Madison, James N. Residence, Warwick. 21. S. Farmer. Enlisted Sept. 28, 1861. Mustered out Oct. 15, 1864.

Mallett, Michael. Residence, Boston, MA. 26. S. Laborer. Enlisted Sept. 18, 1862. Trans. to Co. G, 7th R.I. Vols. Oct. 21, 1864. Mustered out June 9, 1865. Died Feb. 20, 1913. Interred at Washington State Veterans Home, Retsil, WA.

Matthewson, John A. Residence, Coventry. 44. S. Farmer. Enlisted Aug. 8, 1862. KIA Sept. 17, 1862 at Antietam, MD.

Mowry, Benjamin S. Residence, Burrillville. 23. S. Butcher. Enlisted Sept. 9, 1861. Mustered out Oct. 15, 1864. Died 1923. Interred at South Burial Ground, Warren, RI.

Negus, Darius. Residence, Tiverton. 21. M. Farmer. Enlisted Sept. 17, 1861. WIA, left arm amputated, Sept. 17, 1862 at Antietam, MD. Discharged for disability April 23, 1863 at Washington, DC. Died July 17, 1911. Interred at Oak Grove Cemetery, Fall River, MA.

Oakley, John. Residence, Newport. 21. S. Laborer. Enlisted Aug. 7, 1862. Promoted to Corp.

Paine, James H. Residence, Glocester. 25. M. Farmer. Enlisted Sept. 17, 1861. WIA Mar. 14, 1862 at New Bern, NC. Discharged for disability Feb. 1, 1863. Died Mar. 12, 1908. Interred at Rockland Cemetery, Scituate, RI.

Potter, Phillip J. Residence, Glocester. 18. S. Laborer. Enlisted Sept. 9, 1861. CIA July 30, 1864 at the Crater, Petersburg, VA. Trans. to Co. G, 7th R.I. Vols. Nov. 30, 1864.

Quigley, Martin. Residence, Smithfield. 25. S. Laborer. Enlisted Sept. 11, 1861. CIA, Sept. 17, 1862 at Antietam, MD. Released. WIA, shot in left arm, July 30, 1864 at the Crater, Petersburg, VA. Trans. to Co. G, 7th R.I. Vols. Oct. 21, 1864. Mustered out July 13, 1865. Died Jan. 30, 1922. Interred at St. Francis Cemetery, Pawtucket, RI.

Rhodes, Augustus S. Residence, Tiverton. 21. S. Clerk. Enlisted Sept. 17, 1861. WIA, shot in left arm, Sept. 17, 1862 at Antietam, MD. Discharged for disability Oct. 23, 1862 at York, PA. Died 1927. Interred at Prince's Hill Burial Ground, Barrington, RI.

Saunders, Henry Freeman. Residence, Hopkinton. 21. S. Laborer. Enlisted Oct. 3, 1861. MWIA Sept. 17, 1862 at Antietam, MD. DOW Oct. 25, 1862 at Sharpsburg, MD. Interred at Oak Grove Cemetery, Hopkinton, RI.

Shay, John. Residence, Smithfield. 22. S. Laborer. Enlisted Sept. 9, 1861. Promoted to Corp. Sept. 25, 1862.

Smith, George. Residence, Burrillville. 27. S. Laborer. Enlisted Sept. 9, 1861. Deserted in the face of the enemy Sept. 17, 1862 at Antietam, MD.

Smith, Seneca N. Residence, Glocester. 20. S. Laborer. Enlisted Sept. 9, 1861. Promoted to Corp. Sept. 25, 1862.

Smith, Simeon. Residence, Burrillville. 29. S. Laborer. Enlisted Sept. 9, 1861. Discharged for disability Oct. 16, 1861. Died Feb. 4, 1903. Interred at East Thompson Cemetery, Thompson, CT.

Smith, William H. Residence, Burrillville. 28. M. Laborer. Enlisted Sept. 11, 1861. Trans. to Co. G, 7th R.I. Vols. Oct. 21, 1864. Mustered out July 13, 1865. Interred at Elm Grove Cemetery, North Kingstown, RI.

Staples, Albert H. Residence, Smithfield. 19. S. Laborer. Enlisted Sept. 9, 1861. Died of typhoid Jan. 6, 1862 at Alexandria, VA. Interred at Alexandria National Cemetery, Alexandria, VA. Grave 1145.

Staples, Ephraim. Residence, Smithfield. 45. M. Laborer. Enlisted Sept. 9, 1861. Discharged for disability Jan. 21, 1863 at Washington, DC. Died 1881. Interred at Acotes Hill Cemetery, Glocester, RI.

Staples, William H. Residence, Smithfield. 21. S. Laborer. Enlisted Sept. 9, 1861. Discharged for disability Sept. 29, 1862 at Newport News, VA. Died July 12, 1924. Interred at Pascoag Cemetery, Burrillville, RI.

Steere, Albert L. Residence, Smithfield. 21. S. Farmer. Enlisted Sept. 11, 1861. Deserted Aug. 15, 1862 at Fredericksburg, VA.

Steere, Willard. Residence, Burrillville. 21. S. Laborer. Enlisted Sept 9, 1861. MWIA Mar. 14, 1862 at New Bern, NC. DOW Mar. 29, 1862 at New Bern, NC. Interred at Baker Cemetery, Douglas, MA.

Sullivan, Timothy. Residence, Newport. 18. S. Laborer. Enlisted Aug. 7, 1862. Trans. to Co. G, 7th R.I. Vols. Oct. 21, 1864. Mustered out June 9, 1865. Died Sept. 24, 1879. Interred at St. Mary's Cemetery, Newport, RI.

Sweet, Alba. Residence, Glocester. 20. S. Farmer. Enlisted Sept. 11, 1861. Mustered out Oct. 15, 1864. Interred at Pascoag Cemetery, Burrillville, RI.

Sweet, Henry C. Residence, Glocester. 24. S. Laborer. Enlisted Sept. 9, 1861. Promoted to Corp. Nov. 13, 1862.

Sweet, Herbert N. Residence, Smithfield. 18. S. Laborer. Enlisted Sept. 16, 1861. Trans. to Co. G, 7th R.I. Vols. Oct. 21, 1864. Mustered out July 13, 1865. Died April 5, 1904. Interred at Willard Asylum Cemetery, Willard, NY.

Tourtellott, Reuben. Residence, Burrillville. 37. M. Laborer. Enlisted Sept. 9, 1861. Died of typhoid Oct. 31, 1861 at Washington, DC. Interred at Soldier's Home National Cemetery, Washington, DC. Section G, Grave 3763. Cenotaph at Pascoag Cemetery, Burrillville, RI.

Tyler, Archibald. Residence, Coventry. 24. M. Farmer. Enlisted Aug. 4, 1862. Died of typhoid Jan. 26, 1863 at Falmouth, VA. Interred in unmarked grave at Fredericksburg National Cemetery, Fredericksburg, VA. Cenotaph at Knotty Oak Cemetery, Coventry, RI.

Wall, William. Residence, Providence. 21. S. Laborer. Enlisted June 16, 1862. Trans. to Co. G, 7th R.I. Vols. Oct. 21, 1864. Mustered out July 13, 1865. Died July 21 1888. Interred at St. Patrick's Cemetery, Providence, RI.

Watson, Elisha R. Residence, Coventry. 19. S. Farmer. Enlisted Aug. 4, 1862. CIA July 30, 1864 at the Crater, Petersburg, VA. Trans. to Co. G, 7th R.I. Vols. Apr. 2, 1865. Mustered out June 9, 1865. Died April 20, 1939. Interred at Knotty Oak Cemetery, Coventry, RI.

Young, Ellis. Residence, Coventry. 26. M. Carder. Enlisted Aug. 4, 1862. Discharged for disability Feb. 25, 1863. Died Sept. 16, 1889. Interred at Greenwood Cemetery, Coventry, RI.

COMPANY E

Captains

Allen, John A. Residence, Woonsocket. 26. S. Merchant. Commissioned Oct. 2, 1861. Promoted to Maj. Nov. 20, 1861.

Chase, William S. Promoted from 2nd Lt. Co. E, Nov. 20, 1861. WIA, shot in shoulder, Mar. 14, 1862 at New Bern, NC. Discharged for disability July 18, 1862. Interred at Swan Point Cemetery, Providence, RI.

Reynolds, William J. Promoted from 1st Lt. Co. G, Dec. 8, 1862, CIA July 30, 1864 at the Crater, Petersburg, VA. Trans. to Co. B, 7th R.I. Vols. Oct. 21, 1864. Resigned May 15, 1865. Died Aug. 4, 1913. Interred at Elm Grove Cemetery, North Kingstown, RI.

First Lieutenants

Bucklin, James T.P. Promoted from 2nd Lt. Co. A, Nov. 20, 1861. Promoted to Capt. Co. H, April 30, 1862.

Spooner, Henry J. Promoted from 2nd Lt. Co. E, Oct. 5, 1862. Promoted to adjutant Nov. 1, 1862.

Second Lieutenants

Chase, William S. Residence, Providence. 30. S. Clerk. Commissioned Oct. 2, 1861. Promoted to Capt. Co. E, Nov. 20, 1861.

Crowningshield, George F. Promoted from Sgt. Co. I, Nov. 20, 1861. Promoted to 1st Lt. Co. K, Aug. 11, 1862.

Perry, William R. Promoted from Sgt. Co. G, April 10, 1863. Mustered out Oct. 15, 1864. Interred at Riverside Cemetery, Pawtucket, RI.

Spooner, Henry J. Residence, Providence. Attorney. S. 24. Commissioned Aug. 27, 1862. WIA, hit in hip, Sept. 17, 1862 at Antietam, MD. Promoted to 1st Lt. Co. E, Oct. 5, 1862.

First Sergeants

Black, George A. Promoted from Sgt. Nov. 1, 1862. Mustered out Oct. 15, 1864. Interred at Mt. Hope Cemetery, Lander, WY.

Pierce, Edwin A. Promoted from Corp. Mar. 1, 1862. Promoted to 2nd Lt. Co. B, Aug. 11, 1862.

Robinson, Smith P. Residence, Woonsocket. 56. S. Weaver. Reduced to the ranks Mar. 1, 1862.

Sergeants

Black, George A. Residence, Woonsocket. 22. S. Clerk. Enlisted Sept. 10, 1861. Promoted to 1st Sgt. Nov. 1, 1862.

Durphrey, Joseph. Residence, Woonsocket. 24. S. Carpenter. Enlisted Sept. 8, 1861. Trans. to Regular Army Nov. 26, 1861.

Grady, Timothy. Promoted from Pvt. Sept. 20, 1862. WIA, shot in shoulder, July 30, 1864 at the Crater, Petersburg, VA. Mustered out Oct. 15, 1864. Interred at St. Charles Cemetery, Blackstone, MA.

Jenckes, Allen. Promoted from Wagoner. Promoted to 2nd Lt. Co. D, Jan. 13, 1863.

Joslyn, Erastus. Residence, Woonsocket. 25. M. Painter. Enlisted Sept. 8, 1861. Promoted to 2nd Lt. Co. C, Nov. 20, 1861.

McClaren, John. Promoted from Corp. Nov. 1, 1862. Mustered out Oct. 15, 1864.

Parker, John M. Residence, Smithfield. 21. M. Weaver. Enlisted Sept. 8, 1861. WIA, shot in hand, Sept. 17, 1862 at Antietam, MD. Discharged for disability Jan. 12, 1863 at Washington, DC. Reenlisted in 3rd R.I. Cavalry. Died of illness contracted in the service April 15, 1865 at Smithfield, RI. Interred at Slatersville Cemetery, North Smithfield, RI.

Peck, Walter B. Promoted from Corp. Aug. 12, 1862. WIA, right arm amputated, Sept. 17, 1862 at Antietam, MD. Discharged for disability Jan. 5, 1863. Died Jan. 20, 1873. Interred at Union Village Cemetery, North Smithfield, RI.

Stevens, Peter. Promoted from Corp. Dec. 9, 1861. Mustered out Oct. 15, 1864

Corporals

Ballou, Welcome. Promoted from Pvt. Trans. to Co. B, 7th R.I. Vols. Oct. 21, 1864. Mustered out July 13, 1865. Died Feb. 16, 1904. Interred at Ballou-Buffum Lot, Burrillville Cemetery 37, Burrillville, RI.

Cummings, Silas W. Promoted from Pvt. Promoted to QM Sgt. Jan. 13, 1863.

Clancy, Thomas. Promoted from Pvt. Sept. 20, 1862. WIA, shot in shoulder, July 30, 1864 at the Crater, Petersburg, VA. Trans. to Co. B, 7th R.I. Vols. Oct. 21, 1864. Mustered out July 13, 1865.

Jillson, Andrew. Promoted from Pvt. Mar. 1, 1862. WIA, shot in left arm, July 30, 1864 at the Crater, Petersburg, VA. Trans. to Co. B, 7th R.I. Vols. Oct. 21, 1864. Mustered out July 13, 1865. Died 1907. Interred at Wilcox Cemetery, Bellingham, MA.

Kelley, William G. Promoted from Pvt. WIA, shot in left arm, Sept. 17, 1862 at Antietam, MD. Discharged for disability Nov. 29, 1862. Interred at Greenville Cemetery, Smithfield, RI.

Kennedy, Andrew. Residence, Smithfield. 29. M. Operative. Enlisted Sept. 8, 1861. Mustered out Oct. 15, 1864. Died Aug. 24, 1919. Interred at Swan Point Cemetery, Providence, RI.

McClaren, John. Residence, Woonsocket. 21. S. Operative. Enlisted Sept. 8, 1861. Promoted to Sgt. Nov. 1, 1862.

McNally, James. Promoted from Pvt. Dec. 9, 1861. Trans. to Co. B, 7th R.I. Vols. Oct. 21, 1864. Mustered out July 13, 1865. Interred at Togus National Cemetery, Augusta, ME. Grave 2050.

Miller, Henry C. Residence, Woonsocket. 19. S. Laborer. Enlisted Sept. 8, 1861. Deserted at Fredericksburg, VA, Aug. 23, 1862.

Murray, John J. Promoted from Pvt. Nov. 15, 1861. Trans. to Co. B, 7th R.I. Vols. Oct. 21, 1864. Mustered out July 13, 1865.

Peck, Walter B. Residence, Woonsocket. 23. S. Clerk. Enlisted Sept. 8, 1861. Promoted to Sgt. Aug. 12, 1862.

Pierce, Edwin A. Residence, Woonsocket. 29. M. Mason. Enlisted Sept. 8, 1861. Promoted to 1st Sgt. Mar. 1, 1862.

Stevens, Peter. Residence, Smithfield. 22. S. Jeweler. Enlisted Sept. 8, 1861. Promoted to Sgt. Dec. 9, 1861.

Wardell, Henry. Residence, Smithfield. 22. S. Farmer. Enlisted Sept. 8, 1861. Mustered out Oct. 15, 1864.

Musicians

Boyle, John J. Residence, Cumberland. 21. S. Operative. Enlisted Sept. 10, 1861. Trans. to Co. B, 7th R.I. Vols. Oct. 21, 1864. Mustered out July 13, 1865.

Butterfield, Jabez. Trans. from regimental band. Nov. 15, 1861. Mustered out Oct. 15, 1864. Died April 17, 1905. Interred at Northwood Cemetery, Philadelphia, PA.

Wagoner

Jenckes, Allen. Residence, Woonsocket. 24. M. Clerk. Enlisted Sept. 10, 1861. Promoted to Sgt.

Privates

Andrews, George E. Residence, Coventry. 18. S. Farmer. Enlisted Sept. 18, 1861. WIA Mar. 14, 1862 at New Bern, NC. Mustered out Oct. 15, 1864.

Anthony, Samuel H. Residence, Providence. 18. S. Clerk. Enlisted Aug. 30, 1862. Served as clerk at brigade headquarters. Trans. to Co. B, 7th R.I. Vols. Oct. 21, 1864. Mustered out June 21, 1865. Died Dec. 4, 1881. Interred at Swan Point Cemetery, Providence, RI.

Ballou, Gardiner. Residence, Burrillville. 31. S. Farmer. Enlisted Sept. 10, 1861. Mustered out Oct. 15, 1864. Died 1922. Interred at Joseph Esten Lot, Burrillville Cemetery 31, Burrillville, RI.

Ballou, Welcome. Residence, Burrillville. 39. M. Farmer. Enlisted Sept. 10, 1861. Promoted to Corp.

Ballou, Windsor. Residence, Burrillville. 28. M. Farmer. Enlisted Sept. 10, 1861. Deserted Mar. 5, 1863 at Falmouth, VA.

Boyden, Decatur M. Residence, Smithfield. 21. S. Laborer. Enlisted Sept. 10, 1861. Discharged for disability Mar. 10, 1862 at Roanoke Island, NC. Later reenlisted and served in 7th R.I. Vols. Died 1913. Interred at Mt. Auburn Cemetery, Cambridge, MA.

Bullman, Henry W. Residence, Smithfield. 18. S. Laborer. Enlisted Sept. 10, 1861. Mustered out Oct. 15, 1864.

Butterfield, Henry. Residence, Smithfield. 21. M. Weaver. Enlisted Sept. 10, 1861. Deserted in the face of the enemy, Sept. 17, 1862 at Antietam, MD.

Butterfield, Solomon. Residence, Smithfield. 28. M. Farmer. Enlisted Sept. 10, 1861. Deserted Aug. 23, 1862 at Fredericksburg, VA.

Carter, George L. Residence, Smithfield. 21. M. Weaver. Enlisted Sept. 10, 1861. Mustered out Oct. 15, 1864.

Carter, William H. Residence, Smithfield. 23. M. Weaver. Enlisted Sept. 8, 1861. Discharged for disability Oct. 9, 1862 at New York, NY. Died 1913. Interred at Greenwood Cemetery, Coventry, RI.

Chase, Alexander. Residence, Woonsocket. 33. M. Operative. Enlisted Sept. 10, 1861. Discharged for disability Sept. 10, 1862 at Providence, RI. Interred at Oak Hill Cemetery, Bellingham, MA.

Chase, Charles A. Residence, Woonsocket. 19. S. Clerk. Enlisted Sept. 17, 1862. Trans. to Co. B, 7th R.I. Vols. Oct. 21, 1864. Mustered out June 9, 1865. Died Aug. 6, 1911. Interred at Elm Grove Cemetery, North Kingstown, RI.

Clancy, Thomas. Residence, Smithfield. 21. S. Laborer. Enlisted Sept. 10, 1861. WIA, shot in hip, Sept. 17, 1862 at Antietam, MD. Promoted to Corp. Sept. 20, 1862.

Clarence, George. Residence, Smithfield. Enlisted Sept. 10, 1861. Deserted in the face of the enemy Sept. 17, 1862 at Antietam, MD.

Clough, Charles F. Residence, Cumberland. 21. S. Laborer. Enlisted Sept. 8, 1861. Trans. to Co. B, 7th R.I. Vols. Oct. 21, 1864. Mustered out July 13, 1865. Died Dec. 28, 1927. Interred at Greenwood Memorial Terrace, Spokane, WA.

Costigan, Cornelius. Residence, Cumberland. 21. S. Weaver. Enlisted Sept. 8, 1861. KIA Sept. 17, 1862 at Antietam, MD.

Cowley, Thomas. Residence, Woonsocket. 23. S. Weaver. Enlisted Sept. 15, 1861. Discharged for disability Oct. 6, 1862.

Craig, James. Residence, Smithfield. 42. M. Laborer. Enlisted Sept. 8, 1861. Discharged for disability Dec. 10, 1862. Died Oct. 23, 1894. Interred at Slatersville Cemetery, North Smithfield, RI.

Cummings, Silas W. Residence, Burrillville. 18. S. Clerk. Enlisted Sept. 8, 1861. Promoted to Corp.

Cusick, Bernard. Residence, Woonsocket. 21. M. Blacksmith. Enlisted Sept. 8, 1861. WIA Sept. 14, 1862 at South Mountain, MD. WIA, shot in foot, Sept. 17, 1862 at Antietam, MD. Discharged for disability May 1, 1863 at New York, NY.

Davis, Clark E. Residence, Eaton, NH. 21. S. Farmer. Enlisted Sept. 14, 1862. KIA July 30, 1864 at the Crater, Petersburg, VA.

Day, Michael O. Residence, Smithfield. 30. M. Stonecutter. Enlisted Sept. 8, 1861. Mustered out Oct. 15, 1864. Interred at St. John's Cemetery, North Smithfield, RI.

Donnelly, James. Residence, Woonsocket. 22. S. Operative. Enlisted Sept. 19, 1862. Trans. to Co. B, 7th R.I. Vols. Oct. 21, 1864. Mustered out July 13, 1865.

Dunn, James L. Residence, Woonsocket. 18. S. Laborer. Enlisted Aug. 2, 1862 Trans. to Co. B, 7th R.I. Vols. Oct. 21, 1864. Mustered out June 9, 1865.

Dunn, William. Residence, Woonsocket. 21. S. Laborer. Enlisted Aug. 2, 1862. Trans. to Co. B, 7th R.I. Vols. Oct. 21, 1864. Mustered out June 21, 1865.

Ennis, Lawrence. Residence, Woonsocket. 22. M. Operative. Enlisted July 22, 1862. WIA, shot in side, July 30, 1864 at the

Crater, Petersburg, VA. Trans. to Co. B, 7th R.I. Vols. Oct. 21, 1864. Mustered out June 9, 1865. Died July 20, 1890. Interred at St. Charles Cemetery, Blackstone, MA.

Flood, John. Residence, Smithfield. 18. S. Carder. Enlisted Nov. 13, 1862. Trans. to Co. B, 7th R.I. Vols. Oct. 21, 1864. Mustered out July 13, 1865.

Gibbon, Hugh. Residence, Woonsocket. 42. M. Weaver. Enlisted Sept. 8, 1861. Discharged for disability Feb. 19, 1863 at York, PA.

Grady, Timothy. Residence, Smithfield. 22. S. Operative. Enlisted, Sept. 8, 1861. Promoted to Sgt. Sept. 20, 1862.

Greaves, John N. Residence, Smithfield. 22. S. Operative. Enlisted Sept. 8, 1861. Mustered out Oct. 15, 1864. Died Jan. 8, 1922. Interred at Odd Fellows cemetery, Moweaqua, IL.

Griffin, Sylvester. Residence, Smithfield. 21. S. Operative. Enlisted Sept. 9, 1861. Trans to Co. B, 7th R.I. Vols. Oct. 21, 1864. Mustered out July 13, 1865. Died Dec. 19, 1901. Interred at St. Johns Cemetery, Worcester, MA.

Haberlin, John. Residence, Woonsocket. 21. S. Hostler. Enlisted Sept. 8, 1861. Mustered out Oct. 15, 1864. Interred at St. Ann's Cemetery, Cranston, RI.

Hamilton, Robert. Residence, Woonsocket. 26. S. Mariner. Enlisted Sept. 8, 1861. WIA, shot in forehead, July 30, 1864 at the Crater, Petersburg, VA. Trans. to Co. B, 7th R.I. Vols. Oct. 21, 1864. Mustered out July 13, 1865.

Hanover, James. Residence, Smithfield. 21. S. Operative. Enlisted Sept. 8, 1861. Discharged for disability Nov. 3, 1862 at Providence, RI.

Healy, Thaddeus C. Residence, Charlestown. 19. S. Farmer. Enlisted Sept. 8, 1861. Died of diphtheria Aug. 23, 1863 at

Suffolk, VA. Interred at Hampton National Cemetery, Hampton, VA. Section B, Grave 4664.

Hearns, Daniel. Residence, Woonsocket. 25. S. Operative. Enlisted Sept. 8, 1861. Mustered out Oct. 15, 1864.

Hennessey, William. Residence, Woonsocket. 25. S. Operative. Enlisted Sept. 27, 1861. WIA, shot in hip, Sept. 17, 1862 at Antietam, MD. Trans. to Co. B, 7th R.I. Vols. Oct. 21, 1864. Mustered out July 13, 1865. Interred at St. Francis Cemetery, Pawtucket, RI.

Henry, John. Residence, Woonsocket. 21. S. Laborer. Enlisted Sept. 8, 1861. WIA, shot in knee, Dec. 13, 1862 at Fredericksburg, VA. KIA July 27, 1864 at Petersburg, VA. Interred at City Point National Cemetery, Hopewell, VA. Grave 1976.

Hogan, Bernard. Residence, Woonsocket. 22. S. Operative. Enlisted Sept. 8, 1861. Died of small pox Feb. 26, 1864 at Portsmouth, VA. Interred at Hampton National Cemetery, Hampton, VA. Section B, Grave 4662.

Hudson, Samuel. Residence, Woonsocket. 21. S. Operative. Enlisted Sept. 8, 1861. Mustered out Oct. 15, 1864.

Hunt, John. Residence, Smithfield. 18. S. Operative. Enlisted Sept. 8, 1861. WIA, right arm amputated, Sept. 17, 1862 at Antietam, MD. Discharged for disability April 13, 1863 at Sharpsburg, MD.

Jillson, Andrew. Residence, Cumberland. 23. S. Laborer. Enlisted Sept. 8, 1861. Promoted to Corp. Mar. 1, 1862.

Jillson, Hyman E. Residence, Cumberland. 21. S. Farmer. Enlisted Sept. 8, 1861. Mustered out Oct. 15, 1864. Died July 12, 1919. Interred at Oak Hill Cemetery, Woonsocket, RI.

Kelley, Joseph. Residence, Smithfield. 19. S. Operative. Enlisted Sept. 8, 1861. Trans. to Co. B, 7th R.I. Vols. Oct. 21, 1864. Mustered out June 9, 1865.

Kelley, Thomas. Residence, Woonsocket. 19. S. Shoemaker. Enlisted Sept. 8, 1861. Trans. to Co. B, 7th R.I. Vols. Oct. 21, 1864. Mustered out July 13, 1865.

Kelley, William G. Residence, Woonsocket. 25. M. Mason. Enlisted Sept. 19, 1861. Promoted to Corp.

Kennedy, Robert. Residence, Smithfield. 22. S. Operative. Enlisted Sept. 8, 1861. WIA, shot in hand, July 30, 1864 at the Crater, Petersburg, VA. Mustered out Oct. 15, 1864. Died Jan. 8, 1887. Interred at Pascoag Cemetery, Burrillville, RI.

Kennedy, Patrick. Residence, Smithfield. 23. M. Operative. Enlisted Sept. 8, 1861. Discharged for disability Dec. 17, 1862. Died April 21, 1896. Interred at St. Charles Cemetery, Blackstone, MA.

Lynch, Edwin. Residence, Cranston. 23. S. Farmer. Enlisted Nov. 12, 1862. WIA July 8, 1864 at Petersburg, VA. Trans. to Co. B, 7th R.I. Vols. Oct. 21, 1864. Mustered out July 13, 1865.

McNally, James. Residence, Woonsocket. 28. S. Hostler. Enlisted Sept. 8, 1861. Promoted to Corp. Dec. 9, 1861.

McSoley, Michael. Residence, Woonsocket. 22. S. Operative. Enlisted Sept. 18, 1861. Deserted in the face of the enemy Sept. 17, 1862 at Antietam, MD.

Millwood, James. Residence, Woonsocket. 22. S. Operative. Enlisted Sept. 30, 1861. Deserted in the face of the enemy Sept. 17, 1862 at Antietam, MD.

Murray, John J. Residence, Woonsocket. 26. S. Laborer. Enlisted Sept. 8, 1861. Promoted to Corp. Nov. 15, 1861.

Nickerson, Horace M. Residence, Woonsocket. 22. S. Teamster. Enlisted Sept. 8, 1861. Trans. to Co. B, 7th R.I. Vols. Oct. 21, 1864. Mustered out July 13, 1865.

Ormes, Michael. Residence, Woonsocket. 19. S. Teamster. Enlisted Sept. 8, 1861. WIA, shot in hip, Sept. 17, 1862 at Antietam, MD. WIA, shot in left thigh, July 30, 1864 at the Crater, Petersburg, VA. Trans. to Co. B, 7th R.I. Vols. Oct. 21, 1864. Mustered out July 13, 1865.

Pickering, Henry W. Residence, Cumberland. 21. S. Farmer. Enlisted Sept. 8, 1861. Trans. to Co. B, 7th R.I. Vols. Oct. 21, 1864. Mustered out July 13, 1865. Died Nov. 20, 1928. Interred at Wilcox Cemetery, Bellingham, MA.

Pierce, William F. Residence, Woonsocket. 43. M. Laborer. Enlisted Sept. 10, 1862. Trans. to Co. B, 7th R.I. Vols. Oct. 21, 1864. Mustered out June 9, 1865. Died Nov. 30, 1874. Interred at Union Cemetery, North Smithfield, RI.

Potter, Henry M. Residence, Smithfield. 19. S. Laborer. Enlisted Sept. 8, 1861. Trans. to Co. B, 7th R.I. Vols. Oct. 21, 1864. Mustered out July 13, 1865. Died Aug. 29, 1916. Interred at Moshassuck Cemetery, Central Falls, RI.

Regan, John. Residence, Woonsocket. 24. M. Weaver. Enlisted Oct. 30, 1862. Trans. to Co. B, 7th R.I. Vols. Oct. 21, 1864. Mustered out July 13, 1865.

Reynolds, John. Residence, Smithfield. 37. M. Operative. Enlisted Sept. 8, 1861. Deserted in the face of the enemy Sept. 17, 1862 at Antietam, MD.

Riley, Terrence. Residence, Woonsocket. 26. S. Laborer. Enlisted Sept. 8, 1861. Discharged for disability Aug. 9, 1862 at Fredericksburg, VA. Died May 5, 1889. Interred at Togus National Cemetery, Augusta, ME. Grave 1503.

Robinson, Smith P. Reduced from 1st Sgt. Mustered out Oct. 15, 1864. Died 1872. Interred at Acotes Hill Cemetery, Glocester, RI.

Schofield, Joseph. Residence, Whitinsville, MA. 41. M. Machinist. Enlisted Aug. 13, 1862. Trans. to Co. B, 7th R.I. Vols. Oct. 21, 1864. Mustered out June 9, 1865. Died April 12, 1879. Interred at Pine Grove Cemetery, Northbridge, MA.

Shaw, Thomas. Residence, Woonsocket. 21. M. Operative. Enlisted Sept. 8, 1861. Deserted at Fredericksburg, VA. Aug. 23, 1862.

Sheldon, Lowell. Residence, Burrillville. 32. S. Laborer. Enlisted Sept. 8, 1861. Trans. to Co. B, 7th R.I. Vols. Oct. 21, 1864. Died May 20, 1902. Interred at Evergreen Cemetery, Douglas, MA.

Smith, Edwin M. Residence, Smithfield. 18. S. Farmer. Enlisted Sept. 16, 1862. CIA July 30, 1864 at the Crater, Petersburg, VA. Trans. to Co. B, 7th R.I. Vols. Nov. 30, 1864. Mustered out July 13, 1865. Interred at Greenville Cemetery, Smithfield, RI.

Street, Edwin. Residence, Smithfield. 24. M. Weaver. Enlisted Sept. 8, 1861. KIA Mar. 14, 1862 at New Bern, NC.

Sullivan, Martin. Residence, Smithfield. 21. S. Laborer. Enlisted Sept. 19, 1861. Trans. to Co. B, 7th R.I. Vols. Oct. 21, 1864. Mustered out July 13, 1865.

Tyler, Edwin. Residence, Smithfield. 35. M. Laborer. Enlisted Sept. 8, 1861. MWIA, shot in wrist and leg, Sept. 17, 1862 at Antietam, MD. DOW Oct. 13, 1862 at Sharpsburg, MD. Interred at Antietam National Cemetery, Sharpsburg, MD. Rhode Island Section, Grave 2837. Cenotaph at Slatersville Cemetery, North Smithfield, RI.

Vance, Joseph. Residence, Woonsocket. 16. S. Operative. Enlisted Sept. 8, 1861. Mustered out Oct. 15, 1864. Died 1901. Interred at St. Francis Cemetery, Pawtucket, RI.

Warner, James L. Residence, Providence. 18. S. Mariner. Enlisted Sept. 7, 1861. Mustered out Oct. 15, 1864.

Watson, Ferdinand L. Residence, Woonsocket. 18. S. Laborer. Enlisted Sept. 8, 1861. Discharged for disability Nov. 14, 1862 at Baltimore, MD. Died July 28, 1900. Interred at Union Village Cemetery, North Smithfield, RI.

Welch, James. Residence, Smithfield. 18. S. Spinner. Enlisted Nov. 11, 1862. Trans. to Co. B, 7th R.I. Vols. Oct. 21, 1864. Medal of Honor Recipient for heroism July 30, 1864 at the Crater. Mustered out July 13, 1865. Died Dec. 17, 1916. Interred at St. Paul's Cemetery, Blackstone, MA.

Weldon, Henry. Residence, Providence. 27. S. Mechanic. Enlisted Sept. 27, 1861. Trans. to Co. B, 7th R.I. Vols. Oct. 21, 1864. Mustered out July 13, 1865. Interred at Grace Church Cemetery, Providence, RI.

Wilde, George. Residence, Smithfield. 21. M. Machinist. Enlisted Sept. 8, 1861. WIA, shot in left hand, July 30, 1864 at the Crater, Petersburg, VA. Mustered out Oct. 15, 1864. Interred at South Macon Cemetery, Macon, IL.

Wood, Thomas. Residence, Providence. 25. M. Mason. Enlisted Sept. 19, 1861. WIA, shot in left hip, Sept. 17, 1862 at Antietam, MD. Dishonorably discharged by sentence of court martial Nov. 21, 1863.

COMPANY F

Captains

Curtis, George E. Promoted from 1st Lt. Co. F, Nov. 1, 1862. WIA, shot in left knee, Dec. 13, 1862 at Fredericksburg, VA. Dismissed from the service. Dec. 24, 1862. Interred at North Burial Ground, Providence, RI.

Kent, Levi F. Residence, Woonsocket. Commissioned Oct. 30, 1861. Promoted to Maj. Aug. 11, 1862.

Gibbs, Peleg H. Promoted from 1st Lt. Co. F, Sept. 7, 1863. WIA, shot in side, July 30, 1864 at the Crater, Petersburg, VA. Mustered out Oct. 15, 1864. Died May 16, 1868. Interred at Island Cemetery, Newport, RI.

First Lieutenants

Curtis, George E. Promoted from 2nd Lt. Co. F, Aug. 11, 1862. Promoted to Capt. Co. F, Nov. 1, 1862.

Gibbs, Peleg H. Promoted from 2nd Lt. Co. F, Jan. 13, 1863. Promoted to Capt. Co. F, Sept. 7, 1863.

Hall, William F. Promoted from 2nd Lt. Co. F, Nov. 20, 1861. Promoted to Capt. Co. C, Aug. 11, 1862.

Second Lieutenants

Curtis, George E. Promoted from 1st Sgt. Co. F, Nov. 20, 1861. WIA Mar. 14, 1862 at New Bern, NC. Promoted to 1st Lt. Co. F, Aug. 11, 1862.

Gibbs, Peleg H. Promoted from Sgt. Co. G, Aug. 29, 1862. Promoted to 1st Lt. Co. F, Jan. 13, 1863.
White, George R. Promoted from Sgt. Co. G, Jan. 13, 1863. Mustered out Oct. 15, 1864. Died July 7, 1903. Interred at Island Cemetery, Newport, RI.

First Sergeants

Coggeshall, Alexander B. Promoted from Sgt. Nov. 20, 1861. Promoted to Capt. 114th U.S.C.T. 1864. Died Nov. 23, 1881. Interred at Oakwood Cemetery, Austin, TX.

Curtis, George E. Residence, Providence. 27. Enlisted Sept. 12, 1861. Promoted to 2nd Lt. Co. F, Nov. 20, 1861.

Herbert, John C. Promoted from Sgt. Trans. to Co. D, 7th R.I. Vols. Oct. 21, 1864. Mustered out July 13, 1865.

Sergeants

Chase, William T. Residence, Providence. 23. M. Farmer. Enlisted Sept. 14, 1861.WIA, shot in head, July 30, 1864 at the Crater, Petersburg, VA. Trans. to Co. G, 7th R.I. Vols. Oct. 21, 1864. Mustered out July 13, 1865. Died April 18, 1904. Interred at Old North Cemetery, Newport, RI.

Coggeshall, Alexander B. Promoted from Pvt. Promoted to 1st Sgt. Nov. 20, 1861.

Edwards, Henry. Promoted from Corp. WIA July 30, 1864 at the Crater, Petersburg, VA. Mustered out Oct. 15, 1864.

Herbert, John C. Residence, Providence. 26. M. Carpenter. Enlisted Sept. 14, 1861. Promoted to 1st Sgt.

Hunt, Charles H. Residence, Providence. 21. S. Jeweler. Enlisted Sept. 14, 1861. Promoted to 2nd Lt. Co. K, Aug. 11, 1862.

Vaughan, Orsemus M.S. Residence, Westerly. 28. S. Box maker. Enlisted Sept. 17, 1861, WIA, shot in thigh, Sept. 17, 1862 at Antietam, MD. Discharged for disability Jan. 2, 1863.

Weeden, Merchant M. Residence, Providence. 28. S. Carpenter. Enlisted Sept. 14, 1861. Trans. to Co. D, 7th R.I. Vols. Oct. 21, 1864. Mustered out July 13, 1865.

Corporals

Allen, Russell W. Promoted from Pvt. WIA, shot in hand, Sept. 17, 1862 at Antietam, MD. Trans. to Co. G, 7th R.I. Vols. Oct. 21, 1864. Died 1908. Interred at Mineral Spring Cemetery, Pawtucket, RI.

Coggeshall, John. Promoted from Pvt. CIA July 30, 1864 at the Crater, Petersburg, VA. Trans. to Co. D, 7th R.I. Vols. Oct. 21, 1864. Mustered out July 13, 1865. Died July 1, 1914. Interred at Oak Grove Cemetery, Fall River, MA.

Collins, Rhodes T.W. Residence, Warwick. 18. S. Laborer. Enlisted Sept. 23, 1861. Trans. to VRC July 1, 1863. Died Mar. 28, 1882. Interred at Greenwood Cemetery, Coventry, RI.

Earley, Patrick. Promoted from Pvt. Jan. 1, 1864. WIA, shot in ankle, Sept. 17, 1862 at Antietam, MD. WIA, shot in head July 30, 1864 at the Crater, Petersburg, VA. Trans. to Co. G, 7th R.I. Vols. Oct. 21, 1864.

Edwards, Henry. Residence, Providence. Enlisted Sept. 16, 1861. 26. M. Machinist. Promoted to Sgt.

Hayden, Robert. Residence, Providence. 21. S. Jeweler. Enlisted Sept. 14, 1861. Died of typhoid June 12, 1862 at Washington, DC.

McGahey, James. Promoted from Pvt. Trans. to Co. D, 7th R.I. Vols. Oct. 21, 1864. Mustered out July 13, 1865.

Malarkey, Charles. Promoted from Pvt. Trans. to Co. D, 7th R.I. Vols. Oct. 21, 1864. Mustered out July 13, 1865.

Rogers, Isaac H. Promoted from Pvt. Trans. to Co. D, 7th R.I. Vols. Oct. 21, 1864. Mustered out July 13, 1865. Died 1904. Interred at North Burial Ground, Providence, RI.

Musician

Andrews, Israel. Residence, Coventry. 24. M. Teamster. Enlisted Sept. 10, 1861. Mustered out Oct. 15, 1864. Died Nov. 23, 1909. Interred at Pine Grove Cemetery, Coventry, RI.

Wagoner

Latham, Fenner. Residence, Providence. 32. S. Laborer. Enlisted Sept. 14, 1861. Mustered out Oct. 15, 1864. Died Aug. 25, 1898. Interred at North Burial Ground, Providence, RI.

Privates

Allen, Russell W. Residence, Pawtucket. 19. S. Jeweler. Enlisted Sept. 17, 1861. Promoted to Corp.

Bagley, John. Residence, Cranston. 23. M. Operative. Enlisted Sept. 17, 1861. Trans. to Co. D, 7th R.I. Vols. Oct. 21, 1864. Mustered out July 13, 1865. Died Oct. 12, 1915. Interred at St. Mary's Cemetery, West Warwick, RI.

Beaumont, John. Residence, Cumberland. 25. S. Mule spinner. Enlisted Oct. 30, 1862. Trans. to Co. G, 7th R.I. Vols. Oct. 21, 1864. Mustered out July 13, 1865. Interred at Oak Grove Cemetery, Pawtucket, RI.

Bentley, Allen W. Residence, Cranston. 23. M. Operative. Enlisted Sept. 17, 1861. Trans. to Co. G, 7th R.I. Vols. Oct. 21, 1864. Mustered out July 13, 1865.

Brown, John H. Residence, Providence. 19. S. Stone cutter. Enlisted Sept. 16, 1861. Trans. to Co. G, 7th R.I. Vols. Oct. 21, 1864. Mustered out July 13, 1865.

Cady, David E. Residence, Providence. 19. S. Operative. Enlisted Sept. 14, 1861. Deserted in the face of the enemy Sept. 17, 1862 at Antietam, MD.

Carroll, Thomas. Residence, Providence. 29. M. Laborer. Enlisted Sept. 17, 1861. Trans. to Co. G, 7th R.I. Vols. Oct. 21, 1864. Mustered out July 13, 1865.

Caswell, William A. Residence, Warwick. 28. S. Farmer. Enlisted Sept. 13, 1861. Discharged for disability Aug. 11, 1862. Died May 20, 1889. Interred at Greenwood Cemetery, Coventry, RI.

Caughlin, Michael. Residence, Providence. 18. S. Laborer. Enlisted Sept. 17, 1862. Deserted Sept. 10, 1862 near Frederick, MD.

Cavanaugh, Luke. Residence, Providence. 29. M. Laborer. Enlisted Sept. 14, 1861. Discharged for disability Sept. 10, 1862 at Providence, RI.

Clark, John M. Residence, Providence. 18. S. Laborer. Enlisted Sept. 18, 1861. Mustered out Oct. 15, 1864. Died Nov. 5, 1916. Interred at Togus National Cemetery, Augusta, ME. Grave 3477.

Coen, James. Residence, Providence. 33. M. Teamster. Enlisted Sept. 14, 1861. Trans. to Co. G, 7th R.I. Vols. Oct. 21, 1864. Mustered out July 13, 1865. Died May 3, 1883. Interred at Togus National Cemetery, Augusta, ME. Grave 361.

Coggeshall, Alexander B. Residence, Scituate. 18. S. Farmer. Enlisted Sept. 13, 1861. Promoted to Sgt.

Coggeshall, John S. Residence, Tiverton. 18. S. Farmer. Enlisted Sept. 17, 1861. Promoted to Corp.

Coggeshall, Thomas. Residence, Tiverton. 18. S. Farmer. Enlisted Mar. 15, 1864. WIA, shot in right eye, July 30, 1864 at the Crater, Petersburg, VA. Mustered out Oct. 15, 1865.

Cook, James. Residence, Providence. 33. M. Barber. Enlisted Sept. 12, 1861. Mustered out Oct. 15, 1864. Interred at Moshassuck Cemetery, Central Falls, RI.

Corey, John A. Residence, Richmond. 25. S. Laborer. Enlisted Sept. 12, 1861. Trans. to Co. G, 7th R.I. Vols. Oct. 21, 1864. Mustered out July 13, 1865. Died Feb. 4, 1917. Interred at Pine Grove Cemetery, Hopkinton, RI.

Dorman, William. Residence, Providence. 34. M. Laborer. Enlisted Sept. 17, 1861. Trans. to Co. G, 7th R.I. Vols. Oct. 21, 1864. Mustered out July 13, 1865. Died Jan. 11, 1883. Interred at Saints Peter & Paul Cemetery, Coventry, RI.

Douglas, George. Residence, Providence. 18. S. Laborer. Enlisted Sept. 19, 1861. Discharged for disability Sept. 20, 1862. Died 1921. Interred at Hopkins Mills Cemetery, Foster, RI.

Duffy, Michael. Residence, Warwick. 24. S. Laborer. Enlisted Sept. 17, 1861. Trans. to Co. D, 7th R.I. Vols. Oct. 21, 1864. Mustered out July 13, 1865. Died Dec. 27, 1867. Interred at St. Mary's Cemetery, West Warwick, RI.

Earley, Patrick. Residence, Providence. 18. S. Machinist. Enlisted Sept. 13, 1861. Promoted to Corp. Jan. 1, 1864.

Ferrell, Patrick. Residence, Providence. Enlisted Sept. 13, 1861. WIA, right leg amputated, Sept. 17, 1862 at Antietam, MD. Discharged for disability Dec. 1, 1862.

Fieldson, Joseph. Residence, Woonsocket. 21. S. Operative. Enlisted Sept. 14, 1861. Trans. to Co. D, 7th R.I. Vols. Oct. 21, 1864. Mustered out July 13, 1865.

Fieldson, Joshua. Residence, Woonsocket. 44. M. Laborer. Enlisted Sept. 14, 1861. Trans. to Co. D, 7th R.I. Vols. Oct. 21, 1864. Mustered out July 13, 1865.

Fitzgerald, John. Residence, Providence. 18. S. Shoe maker. Enlisted Sept. 9, 1861. Died of typhoid May 9, 1862 at New Bern, NC.

Frisby, Silas. Residence, Cumberland. 18. S. Laborer. Enlisted Sept. 17, 1861. MWIA Mar. 14, 1862 at New Bern, NC. DOW April 3, 1862 at New Bern, NC. Interred at New Bern National Cemetery, New Bern, NC. Section 11, Grave 1864.

Gates, James M. Residence, Providence. 18. S. Farmer. Enlisted Sept. 12, 1861. Trans. to Regular Army Nov. 2, 1862.

Goodwin, John. Residence, Providence. 18. S. Painter. Enlisted Sept. 17, 1861. WIA July 30, 1864 at the Crater, Petersburg, VA. Mustered out Oct. 15, 1864. Interred at St. Francis Cemetery, Pawtucket, RI.

Gladding, Oliver H. Residence, Newport. 19. S. Painter. Enlisted Aug. 12, 1862. Trans. to Co. D, 7th R.I. Vols. Oct. 21, 1864. Mustered out June 9, 1865.

Griffith, Thomas W. Residence, Pawtucket. 27. S. Harness maker. Enlisted Sept. 17, 1861. WIA, shot in jaw, Dec. 13, 1862 at Fredericksburg, VA. Trans. to VRC Oct. 20, 1863.

Grinnell, Edson. Residence, Tiverton. 23. S. Farmer. Enlisted Sept. 23, 1861. Trans. to Co. D, 7th R.I. Vols. Oct. 21, 1864. Mustered out July 13, 1865. Died 1905. Interred at Pleasant View Cemetery, Tiverton, RI.

Harkness, Charles. Residence, Roxbury, MA. 25. S. Brass finisher. Enlisted Oct. 30, 1861. WIA, shot in ankle, Sept. 17, 1862 at Antietam, MD. WIA, shot in right leg, Dec. 13, 1862 at Fredericksburg, VA. Trans. to Co. D, 7th R.I. Vols. Oct. 21, 1864. Mustered out July 13, 1865.

Harrington, Jeremiah. Residence, Ellsworth, ME. 24. M. Carpenter. Enlisted Sept. 17, 1861. Died of typhoid Feb. 16, 1862 at Roanoke, NC. Interred at New Bern National Cemetery, New Bern, NC. Section 11, Grave 1869.

Holland, John. Residence, Johnston. 18. S. Operative. Enlisted Sept. 12, 1861. Trans. to Co. D, 7th R.I. Vols. Oct. 21, 1864. Mustered out July 13, 1865. Interred at St. Francis Cemetery, Pawtucket, RI.

Holley, William. Residence, Providence. 18. S. Laborer. Enlisted Sept. 17, 1861. Trans. to Co. D, 7th R.I. Vols. Oct. 21, 1864. Mustered out July 13, 1865.

Johnson, John F. Residence, Warwick. 21. M. Operative. Enlisted Sept. 17, 1861. WIA Mar. 14, 1862 at New Bern, NC. Discharged for disability Jan. 2, 1863 at Portsmouth, RI. Died of disease contract in the service, August 22, 1863 at Warwick, RI. Interred at Large Maple Root Cemetery, Coventry, RI.

Johnson, Thomas H. Residence, Warwick. 21. S. Operative. Enlisted Sept. 16, 1861. Discharged for disability Oct. 7, 1862. Interred at Veterans Memorial Cemetery, Erie, PA.

Kelley, George W. Residence, Coventry. 22. S. Farmer. Enlisted Sept. 14, 1861. Died of typhoid Dec. 20, 1862 at Falmouth, VA. Interred at Walker-Kelley Cemetery, Coventry Cemetery 14, Coventry, RI.

Kelley, Martin. Residence, Coventry. 25. S. Farmer. Enlisted Sept. 14, 1861. WIA, shot in ankle, Sept. 17, 1862 at Antietam, MD. Mustered out Oct. 15, 1864. Died Sept. 29, 1871. Interred at Walker-Kelley Cemetery, Coventry Cemetery 14, Coventry, RI.

Lawton, Arnold. Residence, Coventry. 37. M. Dyer. Enlisted Sept. 17, 1861. Discharged for disability April 1, 1863. Died Jan. 23, 1907. Interred at Greenwood Cemetery, Coventry, RI.

Luther, George P. Residence, Providence. 18. S. Operative. Enlisted Sept. 5, 1861. Deserted Sept. 4, 1862 at Washington, DC.

McDonald, Charles. Residence, New York, NY. 18. S. Machinist. Mustered out Oct. 15, 1864.

McGahey, James. Residence, Providence. 18. S. Jeweler. Enlisted Sept. 12, 1861. Promoted to Corp.

McGuire, Bernard. Residence, Providence. 27. M. Laborer. Enlisted Sept. 17, 1861. WIA, shot in right shoulder, Sept. 17, 1862 at Antietam, MD. Discharged for disability Mar. 17, 1863.

McShane, Patrick. Residence, Boston, MA. 35. M. Laborer. Trans. to Co. D, 7th R.I. Vols. Oct. 21, 1864. Mustered out July 13, 1865. Died 1886. Interred at St. Mary's Cemetery, West Warwick, RI.

McSheene, John. Residence, Warwick. 35. M. Laborer. Enlisted Aug. 29, 1862. WIA Sept. 14, 1862 at South Mountain, MD. WIA, shot in head, Dec. 13, 1862 at Fredericksburg, VA. Discharged for disability Mar. 7, 1863.

Malarkey, Charles. Residence, Providence. 21. S. Laborer. Enlisted Sept. 17, 1862. Promoted to Corp.

Manchester, Thomas. Residence, Tiverton. 21. S. Farmer. Enlisted Sept. 5, 1861. Died of typhoid Nov. 23, 1862 at Sharpsburg, MD. Interred at Antietam National Cemetery, Sharpsburg, MD. Rhode Island Section, Grave 2839.

Matthewson, William W. Residence, Providence. 23. S. Laborer. Enlisted Sept. 17, 1861. Mustered out Oct. 15, 1864. Interred at Roberts-Matthewson Lot, Cranston Cemetery 16, Cranston, RI.

Morris, Thomas. Residence, Providence. 18. S. Operative. Enlisted Sept. 17, 1861. WIA, left leg amputated, July 30, 1864 at the Crater, Petersburg, VA. Mustered out Oct. 15, 1864.

Munn, Henry. Residence, Hull, MA. 38. S. Farmer. Enlisted Sept. 14, 1861. WIA Mar. 14, 1862 at New Bern, NC. Trans. to VRC Sept. 7, 1863. Died of disease Feb. 3, 1865 at Elmira, NY. Interred at Woodlawn National Cemetery, Elmira, NY. Grave 66.

Nichols, William H. Residence, Smithfield. 29. M. Operative. Enlisted Sept. 17, 1861. Mustered out Oct. 15, 1864. Died May 6, 1911. Interred at Holden-Bicknell-Taylor Lot, Warwick Cemetery 99, Warwick, RI.

O'Donnell, Patrick. Residence, Providence. 31. M. Laborer. Enlisted Sept. 14, 1861. Died of tuberculosis June 14, 1863 at Providence, RI. Interred at St. Patrick's Cemetery, Providence, RI.

Pierce, William F. Residence, Coventry. 41. S. Machinist. Enlisted Sept. 17, 1861. Discharged for disability May 18, 1863. Died Nov. 30, 1874. Interred at Union Village Cemetery, North Smithfield, RI.

Pike, Ephraim. Residence, Warwick. 21. S. Machinist. Enlisted Sept. 17, 1861. KIA Sept. 17, 1862 at Antietam, MD. Interred at Greenwood Cemetery, Coventry, RI.

Riley, Bernard. Residence, Providence. 18. S. Laborer. Enlisted Sept. 12, 1861. Discharged for disability Dec. 7, 1862 at Falmouth, VA.

Rogers, Isaac H. Residence, Providence. 18. S. Baker. Enlisted Sept. 17, 1862. Promoted to Corp.

Russell, James. Residence, Warwick. 18. S. Operative. Enlisted Sept. 17, 1861. WIA, shot in wrist, Sept. 17, 1862 at Antietam, MD. Mustered out Oct. 15, 1864.

Searle, Franklin V. Residence, Charleston, MA. 18. S. Laborer. Enlisted Sept. 17, 1861. Trans. to Co. D, 7th R.I. Vols. Oct. 21, 1864. Mustered out July 13, 1865. Died 1902. Interred at Barden Cemetery, Scituate Cemetery 39, Scituate, RI.

Slocum, George B. Residence, East Greenwich. 18. S. Machinist. Enlisted Sept. 13, 1861. WIA Sept. 17, 1862 at Antietam, MD. Discharged for disability Mar. 10, 1863 at Philadelphia, PA. Died Dec. 9, 1918. Interred at Elmwood Cemetery, Kansas City, MO.

Smith, Alexander. Residence, Foster. 42. M. Operative. Enlisted Sept. 12, 1861. WIA, shot in groin, Sept. 17, 1862 at Antietam, MD. Discharged for disability Nov. 7, 1862 at Baltimore, MD. Died 1864. Interred at Jones-Simmons Lot, Scituate, RI.

Smith, John. Residence, Newport. Enlisted Sept. 12, 1861. Mustered out Oct. 15, 1864. Died of disease contracted in the service Nov. 30, 1864 at Newport, RI. Interred at Island Cemetery, Newport, RI.

Stubbs, Robert. Residence, Boston, MA. 24. S. Laborer. Enlisted Sept. 17, 1861. WIA, left foot amputated, Sept. 17, 1862 at Antietam, MD. Discharged for disability Feb. 6, 1863. Died 1900. Interred at St. Patrick's Cemetery, Providence, RI.

Tanner, Edward B. Residence, Warwick. 34. M. Operative. Enlisted Sept. 17, 1861. Trans. to VRC Oct. 9, 1863. Died April 20, 1900. Interred at Cottrell Cemetery, Scituate, RI.

Tillinghast, Charles E. Residence, Warwick. 18. S. Laborer. Enlisted Sept. 16, 1861. Trans. to Co. D, 7th R.I. Vols. Oct. 21, 1864. Mustered out July 13, 1865. Died Feb. 5, 1908. Interred at Topeka Cemetery, Topeka, KS.

Tripp, Green. Residence, Tiverton. 34. M. Farmer. Enlisted Sept. 17, 1861. WIA, shot through both thighs, Sept. 17, 1862 at Antietam, MD. Discharged for disability April 27, 1863. Died 1896. Interred at Old Lake Cemetery, Tiverton, RI.

Tyrone, Patrick. Residence, Providence. 17. S. Laborer. Enlisted Sept. 12, 1861. WIA Sept. 17, 1862 at Antietam, MD. Discharged for disability Mar. 6, 1863.

Ward, Edward. Residence, Hopkinton. 19. S. Operative. Enlisted Sept. 17, 1861. Discharged for disability Dec. 20, 1862 at Falmouth, VA.

Ward, Willard L. Residence, Hopkinton. 22. S. Shoe maker. Enlisted Sept. 17, 1861. Discharged for disability Dec. 28, 1862 at Falmouth, VA.

Westcott, Samuel B. Residence, Johnston. 27. S. Operative. Enlisted Sept. 17, 1861. Discharged for disability Mar. 19, 1863. Died May. 13, 1909. Interred at Greenwood Cemetery, Coventry, RI.

Whitman, Reuben A. Residence, Warwick. 18. S. Operative. Enlisted Sept. 14, 1861. Trans. to Co. D, 7th R.I. Vols. Oct. 21, 1864. Died of dysentery in Second Division, Ninth Army Corps Hospital, City Point, VA, Mar. 20, 1865. Interred at City Point National Cemetery, Hopewell, VA. Section C, Grave 2190. Cenotaph in Greenwood Cemetery, Coventry, RI.

Wilcox, Elijah R. Residence, Tiverton. 29. M. Carpenter. Enlisted Aug. 15, 1862. Trans. to Co. D, 7th R.I. Vols. Oct. 21, 1864. Mustered out June 9, 1865. Died 1912. Interred at Wilcox Cemetery, Bellingham, MA.

Wood, George M. Residence, Deerfield, MA. 21. S. Farmer. Enlisted Sept. 24, 1861. MWIA, shot in foot, Sept. 17, 1862 at Antietam, MD. DOW Oct. 22, 1862 at Frederick, MD. Interred at Antietam National Cemetery, Sharpsburg Maryland. Rhode Island Section, Grave 2841.

Wood, Henry W. Residence, Providence. 17. S. Student. Enlisted Sept. 16, 1861. WIA Sept. 17, 1862 at Antietam, MD. Trans. to Co. D, 7th R.I. Vols. Oct. 21, 1864. Died Sept. 2, 1896. Interred at Pocasset Cemetery, Cranston, RI.

Young, James. Residence, Scituate. 27. M. Teamster. Enlisted Sept. 16, 1861. Mustered out Oct. 15, 1864. Interred at Lakeside-Carpenter Cemetery, East Providence, RI.

COMPANY G

Captains

Andrews, Dennis P. Promoted from 1st Lt. Co. H, Dec. 16, 1862. Resigned Mar. 31, 1863. Died 1896. Interred at West Rockport Cemetery, Rockport, ME.

Bowen, Caleb T. Trans. from Co. I, Aug. 13, 1863. CIA July 30, 1864 at the Crater, Petersburg, VA. Released and Trans. to Co. G, 7th R.I. Vols. Mar. 10, 1865. Mustered out July 13, 1865. Died Dec. 9, 1906. Interred at Lone Fir Pioneer Cemetery, Portland, OR.

Church, Isaac M. Residence, South Kingstown. 48. M. Minister. Promoted from 1st Lt. Co. E, 2nd R.I. Vols. Oct. 8, 1862. Formerly prisoner of war, captured at Bull Run, July 21, 1861. Discharged for disability Dec. 27, 1862. "His health was impaired by his captivity, and he never fully recovered his former strength." Died of illness contracted in the service Oct. 27, 1874 at North Kingstown, RI. Interred at Riverside Cemetery, South Kingstown, RI.

Hopkins, Israel M. Promoted from 1st Lt. Co. G, Nov. 20, 1861. Resigned Aug. 11, 1862. Died July 8, 1887. Interred at Swan Point Cemetery, Providence, RI.

Tew, George W. Residence, Newport. 40. M. Mason. Commissioned Sept. 15, 1861. Promoted to Maj. Nov. 20, 1861.

First Lieutenants

Hopkins, Israel M. Residence, Providence. Commissioned Oct. 30, 1861. Promoted to Capt. Co. G, Nov. 20, 1861.

Munroe, Charles W. Promoted from 2nd Lt. Co. G, Nov. 20, 1861. Resigned Aug. 11, 1862. Died Mar. 20, 1868. Interred at North Burial Ground, Providence, RI.

Reynolds, William J. Promoted from Sgt. Co. H, Dec. 12, 1862. Promoted to Capt. Co. E, Dec. 8, 1862.

Pierce, Edwin A. Promoted from 2nd Lt. Co. B, Feb. 18, 1863 Mustered out Oct. 15, 1864. Died Feb. 1, 1898. Interred at Oak Hill Cemetery, Woonsocket, RI.

Second Lieutenants

Brown, Jeremiah. Residence, Newport. Commissioned Oct. 1, 1861. Resigned Nov. 20, 1861. Interred at Island Cemetery, Newport, RI.

Clarke, Joshua Perry. Promoted from 1st Sgt., Aug. 11, 1862. WIA, shot in chest, Sept. 17, 1862 at Antietam, MD. Discharged for disability Jan. 1, 1863. Died April 11, 1915. Interred at Island Cemetery, Newport, RI.

Munroe, Charles W. Promoted from 1st Sgt. Co. C, Oct. 11, 1861. Promoted to 1st Lt. Co. G, Nov. 20, 1861.

Olney, William C. Promoted from Sgt. Co. I, Jan. 12, 1863. Mustered out Oct. 15, 1864. Died of disease contracted in the service June 20, 1867 at Providence, RI. Interred at North Burial Ground, Providence, RI.

Smith, Jabez S. Promoted from 1st Sgt. Co. G, Nov. 20, 1861. Resigned Aug. 11, 1862. Interred at Island Cemetery, Newport, RI.

First Sergeants

Clarke, Joshua Perry. Promoted from Corp. Nov. 20, 1861. Promoted to 2nd Lt. Co. G, Aug. 11, 1862.

Smith, Jabez S. Residence, Newport. 21. S. Painter. Enlisted Sept. 5, 1861. Promoted to 2nd Lt. Co. G, Nov. 20, 1861.

Townsend, Job. Promoted from Corp. Aug. 11, 1862. Mustered out Oct. 15, 1864. Died Dec. 6, 1918. Interred at Riverside Cemetery, New Bedford, MA.

Sergeants

Barker, William H. Promoted from Corp. Mustered out Oct. 15, 1864. Died Feb. 25, 1914. Interred at Common Burial Ground, Newport, RI.

Gardiner, Gustavus B. Residence, Newport. 19. S. Mason. Enlisted Sept. 11, 1861. KIA Sept. 17, 1862 at Antietam, MD. Interred at Island Cemetery, Newport, RI.

Gibbs, Peleg H. Promoted from Corp. Promoted to 2nd Lt. Co. F, Aug. 29, 1862.

Groff, Charles E. Promoted from Pvt. Oct. 1, 1862. Trans. to Co. G 7th R.I. Vols. Oct. 21, 1864. Died 1906. Interred at North Burial Ground, Newport, RI.

Hornsby, William H. Promoted from Pvt. WIA, shot in hip, Sept. 17, 1862 at Antietam, MD. Discharged for disability Mar. 22, 1863 at Providence, RI.

Lake, Benjamin F. Promoted from Corp. Discharged for disability Aug. 25, 1862 at New Bern, NC. Died Dec. 7, 1902. Interred at Locust Grove Cemetery, Providence, RI.

McCarty, Michael. Promoted from Pvt. May 1, 1864. Mustered out Oct. 15, 1864. Died Nov. 1, 1871. Interred at St. Francis Cemetery, Pawtucket, RI.

Peabody, Frederick J. Promoted from Corp. Aug. 12, 1862. KIA Sept. 30, 1864 at Poplar Spring Church, VA. Interred at Common Burial Ground, Newport, RI.

Perry, William R. Residence, Newport. 23. S. Carpenter. Enlisted Sept. 11, 1861. Promoted to 2nd Lt. Co. E, April 10, 1863.

White, George R. Residence, Newport. 22. S. Porter. Enlisted Sept. 11, 1861. Promoted to 2nd Lt. Co. F, Jan. 13, 1863.

Corporals

Allen, George W. Promoted from Pvt. Oct. 14, 1862. WIA, shot in thigh, May 3, 1863 near Suffolk, VA. Mustered out Oct. 15, 1864. Died 1907. Interred at Middletown Cemetery, Middletown, RI.

Arnold, Horace W. Promoted from Pvt. Oct. 14, 1862. Mustered out Oct. 15, 1864. Died 1914. Interred at Cedar Cemetery, Jamestown Cemetery 5, Jamestown, RI.

Barker, William H. Promoted from Pvt. Oct. 14, 1862. Promoted to Sgt.

Bowman, John. Promoted from Pvt. Jan. 7, 1863. Mustered out Oct. 15, 1864. Interred at Island Cemetery, Newport, RI.

Burdick, Albert N. Residence, Newport. 25. M. Carpenter. Enlisted Sept. 11, 1861. Promoted to 1st Sgt. Co. K, Dec. 8, 1861.

Clarke, Joshua Perry. Residence, Newport. 26. S. Merchant. Enlisted Sept. 13, 1861. Promoted to 1st Sgt. Nov. 20, 1861.

Curtis, Charles S. Residence, South Kingstown. 22. S. Seaman. Enlisted Sept. 11, 1861. Mustered out Oct. 15, 1864. Died 1922. Interred at Braman Cemetery, Newport, RI.

Denham, William S. Promoted from Pvt. Died of typhoid April 18, 1862 at Carolina City, NC. Interred at New Bern National Cemetery, New Bern, NC. Section 11, Grave 1875.

Fish, Bennett J. Promoted from Pvt. Mustered out Oct. 15, 1864.

Gibbs, Peleg H. Residence, Newport. 28. M. Mason. Enlisted Sept. 10, 1861. Promoted to Sgt.

Gibson, John. Promoted from Pvt. Dec. 1, 1862. Mustered out Oct. 15, 1864. Died May 26, 1918. Interred at Oak Ridge Cemetery, Chicago, IL.

Heath, Calvin W. Residence, Newport. 21. S. Merchant. Enlisted Sept. 11, 1861. Discharged for disability Sept. 24, 1862. Interred at Braman Cemetery, Newport, RI.

Lake, Benjamin F. Residence, Newport.28. S. Laborer. Enlisted Sept. 11, 1861. Promoted to Sgt.

Peabody, Frederick J. Residence, Newport. 22. M. Carpenter. Enlisted Sept. 11, 1861. Promoted to Sgt. Aug. 12, 1862.

Sutherland, Andrew. Promoted from Pvt. Trans. to Co. G, 7th R.I. Vols. Oct. 21, 1864. Mustered out July 13, 1865. Died Sept. 10, 1902. Interred at Island Cemetery, Newport, RI.

Tanner, Thomas B. Promoted from Pvt. Served as Regimental Color Bearer. KIA Sept. 17, 1862 at Antietam, MD. Interred at Island Cemetery, Newport, RI.

Townsend, Job. Residence, Newport. 23. S. Carpenter. Enlisted Sept. 11, 1861. Promoted to 1st Sgt. Aug. 11, 1862.

Weeden, Daniel W. Promoted from Pvt. WIA, shot in back, July 30, 1864 at the Crater, Petersburg, VA. Trans. to Co. G, 7th R.I. Vols. Oct. 21, 1864. Mustered out July 13, 1865. Died Mar. 4, 1873. Interred at Holy Cross Episcopal Cemetery, Middletown, RI.

Musicians

Smith, Albert G. Residence, Groton, CT. 18. S. Painter. Enlisted Sept. 11, 1861. Mustered out Oct. 15, 1864. Interred at Common Burial Ground, Newport, RI.

Williams, Robert. Residence, Newport. 21. S. Seaman. Enlisted Sept. 11, 1861. Died of typhoid April 19, 1862 at Beaufort, NC. Interred at Common Burial Ground, Newport, RI.

Wagoners

Boss, Daniel A. Residence, Newport. 21. M. Teamster. Enlisted Sept. 11, 1861. Died of typhoid May 26, 1862 at Beaufort, NC. Interred at Common Burial Ground, Newport, RI.

Watson, Benjamin. Residence, Newport. 19. S. Sailor. Enlisted Sept. 11, 1861. Mustered out Oct. 15, 1864.

Privates

Alger, Edwin G.S. Residence, Newport. 20. M. Painter. Enlisted Sept. 11, 1861. Served in ambulance corps. Mustered out Oct. 15, 1864. Died July 6, 1900. Interred at Island Cemetery, Newport, RI.

Allen, George W. Residence, South Kingstown. 24. M. Carpenter. Enlisted Sept. 11, 1861. Promoted to Corp. Oct. 14, 1862.

Arnold, Horace W. Residence, Middletown. 22. S. Farmer. Enlisted Sept. 11, 1862. Promoted to Corp. Oct. 14, 1862.

Babcock, George M. Residence, Providence. 20. S. Moulder. Enlisted May 15, 1862. Trans. to Co. G, 7th R.I. Vols. Oct. 21,

1864. Mustered out at Alexandria, VA, May 14, 1865. Interred at Swan Point Cemetery, Providence, RI.

Barker, Noah. Residence, Newport. 27. M. Blacksmith. Enlisted Sept. 11, 1861. Mustered out Oct. 15, 1864. Died Nov. 4, 1889. Interred at North Cemetery, Newport, RI.

Barker, William H. Residence, Newport. 21. S. Blacksmith. Enlisted Sept. 11, 1861. Promoted to Corp. Oct. 14, 1862.

Barlow, William H. Residence, Newport. 22. S. Painter. Enlisted Sept. 11, 1861. Discharged for disability Feb. 8, 1863 at Newport News, VA. Interred at Common Burial Ground, Newport, RI.

Boss, Benjamin F. Residence, Newport. 26. S. Farmer. Enlisted Sept. 11, 1861. Discharged for disability Aug. 19, 1862 at Fort Monroe, VA. Died Feb. 1, 1912. Interred at North Cemetery, Newport, RI.

Bowman, John. Residence, Newport. 35. M. Laborer. Enlisted Sept. 11, 1861. Promoted to Corp. Jan. 7, 1863.

Brady, John F. Residence, Newport. 22. S. Sailor. Enlisted Sept. 11, 1861. Discharged for disability Dec. 2, 1862 at Providence, RI. Interred at St. Charles Cemetery, Blackstone, MA.

Cain, Hugh. Residence, Newport. 25. M. Laborer. Enlisted Sept. 11, 1861. Mustered out Oct. 15, 1864.

Carr, David V. Residence, Newport. 21. S. Farmer. Enlisted Sept. 11, 1861. Mustered out Oct. 15, 1864.

Carr, William H. Residence, Newport. 23. S. Farmer. Enlisted Sept. 11, 1861. Died of typhoid June 14, 1862 at Beaufort, NC.

Chase, James S. Residence, Newport. 20. S. Sailor. Enlisted Sept. 11, 1861. WIA, shot in hip, Sept. 17, 1862 at Antietam, MD. Discharged for disability Feb. 5, 1863 at Washington, DC. Died Jan. 10, 1893. Interred at Swan Point Cemetery, Providence, RI.

Chase, John W. Residence, Newport. 20. S. Farmer. Enlisted Sept. 11, 1861. Died of typhoid April 26, 1862 at Carolina City, NC. Interred at New Bern National Cemetery, New Bern, NC. Section 11, Grave 1876.

Clark, Thomas C. Residence, Newport. 22. M. Laborer. Enlisted Sept. 11, 1861. Discharged for disability Nov. 14, 1862. Died 1889. Interred at Braman Cemetery, Newport, RI.

Cornell, Oscar. Residence, Newport. 23. S. Grocer. Enlisted Sept. 11, 1861. Trans. to VRC Aug. 8, 1863. Died April 6, 1923. Interred at Oak Grove Cemetery, Fall River, MA.

Cozzens, John R. Residence, Newport. 23. S. Seaman. Enlisted Sept. 11, 1861. WIA, shot in groin, Sept. 17, 1862 at Antietam, MD. Discharged for disability Feb. 11, 1863 at Portsmouth, RI.

Curtis, Charles S. Residence, South Kingstown. 19. S. Clerk. Enlisted Sept. 11, 1861. Mustered out Oct. 15, 1864. Died 1922. Interred at Braman Cemetery, Newport, RI.

Curtis, Samuel. Residence, South Kingstown. 19. S. Clerk. Enlisted Sept. 11, 1861. Died of typhoid Aug. 20, 1862 at Portsmouth, RI. Interred at Riverside Cemetery, South Kingstown, RI.

Dawley, Benjamin H. Residence, Newport. 21. S. Mason. Enlisted Sept. 11, 1861. WIA, shot in ankle, Sept. 17, 1862 at Antietam, MD. Discharged for disability Nov. 20, 1862 at Baltimore, MD. Died 1924. Interred at Braman Cemetery, Newport, RI.

Denham, William P. Residence, Newport. 18. S. Carpenter. Enlisted Sept. 11, 1861. Trans. to the U.S. Navy May 12, 1864.

Denham, William S. Residence, Newport. 18. S. Seaman. Enlisted Sept. 11, 1861. Promoted to Corp.

Dunnegan, Henry. Residence, Newport. 20. S. Carpenter. Enlisted Sept. 11, 1861. Killed in building collapse Nov. 28, 1863 at Portsmouth, VA. Interred at Hampton National Cemetery, Hampton, VA. Section B, Grave 4654.

Edgar, Algernon H. Residence, Newport. 18. M. Laborer. Enlisted Sept. 11, 1861. Mustered out Oct. 15, 1864. Died 1924. Interred at Oak Grove Cemetery, Pawtucket, RI.

Fish, Bennett J. Residence, Portsmouth. 19. S. Farmer. Enlisted Sept. 11, 1861. Promoted to Corp.

Fish, Henry. Residence, Newport. 31. M. Operative. Enlisted Sept. 12, 1861. KIA Sept. 17, 1862 at Antietam, MD. Interred at Antietam National Cemetery, Sharpsburg, MD. Rhode Island Section, Grave 2824. Cenotaph at Oakland Cemetery, Cranston, RI.

Freeborn, John. Residence, Newport. 19. S. Carpenter. Enlisted Aug. 1, 1862. Trans. to Co. G 7th R.I. Vols. Oct. 21, 1864. Mustered out June 9, 1865.

Freeborn, Thomas M. Residence, Newport. 23. S. Machinist. Enlisted Sept. 11, 1861. Mustered out Oct. 15, 1864. Died July 1, 1901. Interred at Common Burial Ground, Newport, RI.

Freelove, Hiram R. Residence, Newport. 23. M. Baker. Enlisted Sept. 11, 1861. WIA, shot in leg, Dec. 13, 1862 at Fredericksburg, VA. Trans. to VRC Feb. 8, 1863. Interred at Oak Grove Cemetery, Fall River, MA.

Gibson, John. Residence, Providence. 20. S. Mason. Enlisted Sept. 11, 1861. Promoted to Corp. Dec. 1, 1862.

Groff, Charles E. Residence, Newport. 21. S. Carpenter. Enlisted Sept. 11, 1861. Promoted to Sgt. Oct. 1, 1862.

Gordon, Henry W. Residence, Coventry. 29. S. Farmer. Enlisted Aug. 7, 1862. Trans. to Co. G, 7th R.I. Vols. Oct. 21, 1864. Died of disease at Fort Schuyler Hospital, NY, Feb. 1, 1865.

Hogan, James B. Residence, Newport. 30. M. Sail maker. Enlisted Sept. 11, 1861. Mustered out Oct. 15, 1864. Interred at Island Cemetery, Newport, RI.

Hornsby, William H. Residence, Newport. 23. S. Seaman. Enlisted Sept. 17, 1861. Promoted to Sgt.

Hunnewell, William H. Residence, Newport.53. M. Seaman. Enlisted Sept. 11, 1861. Discharged for disability Jan. 22, 1863. Died Sept. 22, 1876. Interred at Mt. Auburn Cemetery, Cambridge, MA.

Kelley, Malachi. Residence, Newport. 18. S. Laborer. Enlisted Aug. 8, 1862. Trans. to Co. G, 7th R.I. Vols. Oct. 21, 1864. Mustered out June 9, 1865.

Ingham, William. Residence, Newport. 19. S. Carpenter. Enlisted Sept. 17, 1861. Mustered out Oct. 15, 1864. Died Aug. 6, 1910. Interred at Pocasset Cemetery, Cranston, RI.

Lake, Israel F. Residence, Newport. 31. S. Clerk. Enlisted Sept. 11, 1861. Mustered out Oct. 15, 1864. Died Nov. 26, 1870. Interred at Island Cemetery, Newport, RI.

Lake, Thomas O. Residence, Newport. 22. S. Plumber. Enlisted Sept. 11, 1861. WIA, shot in shoulder, Dec. 13, 1862 at Fredericksburg, VA. MWIA July 23, 1864 at Petersburg, VA. DOW Aug. 1, 1864 at Washington, DC. Interred at Island Cemetery, Newport, RI.

Landers, James H. Residence, Newport. 21. S. Painter. Enlisted Sept. 11, 1861. KIA Sept. 30, 1864 at Poplar Spring Church, VA. Interred at Island Cemetery, Newport, RI.

Langley, Caleb. Residence, Newport. 39. M. Laborer. Enlisted Sept. 11, 1861. WIA, shot in both legs, Sept. 17, 1862 at Antietam, MD. Discharged for disability Mar. 4, 1863 at Frederick, MD. Died Feb. 27, 1891. Interred at North Cemetery, Newport, RI.

Lawton, Thomas S. Residence, Newport. 31. M. Blacksmith. Enlisted Sept. 11, 1861. Mustered out Oct. 15, 1864. Died 1903. Interred at North Cemetery, Newport, RI.

Lawton, William H. H. Residence, Newport. 21. S. Fisherman. Enlisted Sept. 11, 1861. Discharged for disability Jan. 8, 1864. Interred at North Cemetery, Newport, RI.

Leddy, John. Residence, Newport. 22. S. Laborer. Enlisted Aug. 7, 1862. MWIA Sept. 30, 1864 at Poplar Spring Church, VA. DOW Oct. 18, 1864 at Washington, DC. Interred at Arlington National Cemetery, Arlington, VA. Section 13, Grave 8320.

Luther, Henry A. Residence, Newport. 22. S. Farmer. Enlisted Sept. 15, 1861. Mustered out Oct. 15, 1864. Died Dec 3, 1902. Interred at Pocasset Cemetery, Cranston, RI.

McCarty, Jeremiah. Residence, Newport. 21. S. Seaman. Enlisted Sept. 11, 1861. Trans. to Co. G 7th R.I. Vols. Oct. 21, 1864. Mustered out July 13, 1865.

McCarty, Michael. Residence, Newport. 23. M. Harness maker. Enlisted Sept. 11, 1861. Promoted to Sgt. May 1, 1864.

Markham, James. Residence, Newport. 32. S. Moulder. Enlisted Sept. 11, 1861. Trans. to Co. G 7th R.I. Vols. Oct. 21, 1864.

Mason, Seabury. Residence, Warren. 28. S. Seaman. Enlisted Sept. 11, 1861. WIA, shot in hand, Sept. 17, 1862 at Antietam, MD. Discharged for disability Feb. 12, 1863 at New York, NY.

Mason, William. Residence, Newport. 22. S. Seaman. Enlisted Aug. 16, 1862. Trans. to Co. G 7th R.I. Vols. Oct. 21, 1864.

Mustered out June 9, 1865. Interred at Union Village Cemetery, North Smithfield, RI.

Matthewson, William. Residence, Mendon, MA. 38. M. Seaman. Enlisted Aug. 16, 1862. Trans. to U.S. Navy May 13, 1864.

Murphy, Patrick. Residence, Newport. 19. S. Laborer. Enlisted Sept. 4, 1861. Trans. to Co. G 7th R.I. Vols. Oct. 21, 1864. Mustered out July 13, 1865. Died 1891. Interred at St. Mary's Cemetery, Newport, RI.

Oakley, George. Residence, Newport. 23. S. Painter. Enlisted Sept. 11, 1861. Mustered out Oct. 15, 1864. Died Oct. 24, 1917. Interred at Carpenter Cemetery, East Providence, RI.

Peabody, Edwin H. Residence, Newport. 21. M. Carpenter. Enlisted Sept. 11, 1861. Mustered out Oct. 15, 1864.

Peabody, Frank D. Residence, Newport. 18. S. Cabinet maker. Enlisted Sept. 11, 1861. Discharged for disability July 24, 1863. Died of disease contracted in the service Sept. 13, 1863 at Newport, RI. Interred at Island Cemetery, Newport, RI.

Peckham, Richard H. Residence, Middletown. 41. M. Farmer. Enlisted Sept. 11, 1861. Discharged for disability Sept. 21, 1862 at Beaufort, NC. Died Mar. 31, 1894. Interred at Island Cemetery, Newport, RI.

Phillips, Andrew P. Residence, North Kingstown. 18. S. Laborer. Enlisted Aug. 7, 1862. WIA, shot in shoulder, July 30, 1864 at the Crater, Petersburg, VA. Trans. to Co. G, 7th R.I. Vols. Oct. 21, 1865. Mustered out June 9, 1865. Died 1920. Interred at Greenwood Cemetery, Coventry, RI.

Reardon, Patrick. Residence, Newport. 22. S. Laborer. Enlisted Sept. 11, 1861. WIA, shot in arm, Sept. 17, 1862 at Antietam, MD. Trans. to Co. B 7th R.I. Vols. Oct. 21, 1865. Mustered out July 13, 1865.

Scott, Luke. Residence, Newport. 36. S. Sailor. Enlisted Sept. 11, 1861. WIA, shot in leg, May 3, 1863 near Suffolk, VA. Mustered out Oct. 15, 1864. Died April 11, 1906. Interred at Braman Cemetery, Newport, RI.

Sharkey, Thomas. Residence, Newport. 23. M. Teamster. Enlisted Sept. 11, 1861. Mustered out Oct. 15, 1864.

Shaw, George C. Residence, Newport. 16. M. Laborer. Enlisted Sept. 11, 1861. Trans. to Co. G, 7th R.I. Vols. Oct. 21, 1864. Died 1917. Interred at Island Cemetery, Newport, RI.

Sherman, George H. Residence, Newport.30. S. Gardiner. Enlisted Sept. 11, 1861. WIA, shot in leg, July 30, 1864 at the Crater, Petersburg, VA. Mustered out Oct. 15, 1864. Died May 6, 1901. Interred at Portsmouth Cemetery, Portsmouth, RI.

Spencer, George I. Residence, Newport. 31. M. Clerk. Enlisted Aug. 16, 1862. Trans. to VRC Dec. 18, 1863.

Spooner, Lovell T. Residence, Newport. 22. S. Weaver. Enlisted Aug. 7, 1862. Trans. to Co. G, 7th R.I. Vols. Oct. 21, 1864. Mustered out June 9, 1865.

Stafford, William H. Residence, Cranston. 18. S. Laborer. Enlisted Aug. 7, 1862. Died of dysentery May 23, 1864 at Cranston, RI. Interred at Greenwood Cemetery, Coventry, RI.

Sullivan, John. Residence, Newport. 27. S. Tin man. Enlisted Sept. 11, 1861. Mustered out Oct. 15, 1864. Died Sept. 6, 1894. Interred at Island Cemetery, Newport, RI.

Sutherland, Andrew. Residence, Newport. 23. M. Shoe maker. Enlisted Aug. 12, 1862. Promoted to Corp.

Tanner, Thomas B. Residence, Newport. Enlisted Sept. 11, 1861. 21. S. Laborer. Promoted to Corp.

Taylor, James B. Residence, Newport. 22. S. Laborer. Enlisted Sept. 11, 1861. Discharged for disability Jan. 22, 1863.

Taylor, Samuel. Residence, Newport. 19. S. Seaman. Enlisted Sept. 11, 1861. Discharged for disability June 30, 1863 at New York, NY. Died Mar. 19, 1902. Interred at North Burial Ground, Providence, RI.

Teft, Charles. Residence, Westerly. 25. M. Grocer. Enlisted Aug. 12, 1862. Discharged for disability Feb. 2, 1864 at Portsmouth, RI. Died 1900. Interred at Pocasset Cemetery, Cranston, RI.

Tew, Richard T. Residence, Newport. 27. S. Laborer. Enlisted Sept. 11, 1861. Died of diphtheria Aug. 3, 1863 at Suffolk, VA. Interred at Hampton National Cemetery, Hampton, VA. Section B, Grave 4658.

Walker, James. Residence, Middletown. 24. M. Laborer. Enlisted Sept. 11, 1861. MWIA, shot in stomach, Sept. 17, 1862 at Antietam, MD. DOW Dec. 11, 1862 at Baltimore, MD. Interred at Common Burial Ground, Newport, RI.

Weaver, Alton J. Residence, Middletown. Enlisted Sept. 11, 1861. Died of typhoid Sept. 17, 1862 at New York, NY. Interred at Island Cemetery, Newport, RI.

Weeden, Daniel W. Residence, Jamestown. 27. M. Farmer. Enlisted Sept. 11, 1861. Promoted to Corp.

Williams, John W. Residence, Providence. 18. S. Laborer. Enlisted Sept. 11, 1861. WIA, shot in left thigh, July 30, 1864 at the Crater, Petersburg, VA. Trans. to Co. G, 7th R.I. Vols. Oct. 21, 1864. Mustered out July 13, 1865. Died of dysentery contracted in the service at North Kingstown, RI, Oct. 14, 1865. Interred at Elm Grove Cemetery, North Kingstown, RI.

Williams, George C. Residence, Providence. 30. M. Laborer. Enlisted Sept. 11, 1861. Trans. to U.S. Navy June 3, 1862.

Wood, Nathan. Residence, Newport. 21. S. Seaman. Enlisted Aug. 16, 1862. Trans. to the U.S. Navy May 13, 1864. Died July 29, 1904. Interred at Common Burial Ground, Newport, RI.

Young, William J. Residence, Newport. 21. S. Carpenter. Enlisted Sept. 11, 1861. Mustered out Oct. 15, 1864.

COMPANY H

Captains

Bucklin, James T.P. Promoted from 1st Lt. Co. E, April 30, 1862. Promoted to Maj. Jan. 9, 1863.

Lyons, James W. Promoted from 1st Lt. Co. B, May 23, 1863. On staff duty at 10th Corps headquarters until mustered out Oct. 15, 1864. Interred at Oak Woods Cemetery, Chicago, IL.

Tillinghast, Charles. Residence, Providence. 30. S. Commissioned Sept. 13, 1861. KIA Mar. 14, 1862 at New Bern, NC. Interred at Swan Point Cemetery, Providence, RI.

First Lieutenants

Andrews, Dennis P. Promoted from 2nd Lt. Co. H, Aug. 15, 1862. Promoted to Capt. Co. G, Dec. 16, 1862.

Bowen, Caleb T. Promoted from 2nd Lt. Co. H, Nov. 20, 1861. Promoted to Capt. Co. I, Aug. 11, 1862.

Tillinghast, Albert G. Promoted from Sgt. Co. A, Nov. 1, 1862. WIA, shot in head, July 30, 1864 at the Crater, Petersburg, VA. Mustered out Oct. 15, 1864. Died Feb. 23, 1897. Interred at North Burial Ground, Providence, RI.

Second Lieutenants

Andrews, Dennis P. Promoted from 1st Sgt. Co. D, May 4, 1862. Promoted to 1st Lt. Co. H, Aug. 15, 1862.

Bowen, Caleb T. Residence, North Kingstown. 28. M. Merchant. Commissioned Sept. 13, 1861. Promoted to 1st Lt. Co. H, Nov. 20, 1861.

Harback, Erastus. Promoted from 1st Sgt. Co. H, Nov. 20, 1861. Resigned April 8, 1862. Died Mar. 18, 1916. Interred at Lakeview Cemetery, Upton, MA.

Wilson, Charles. Promoted from Sgt. Co. A, Jan. 13, 1863. Mustered out Oct. 15, 1864.

First Sergeants

Harback, Erastus W. Residence, North Kingstown. 25. M. Painter. Enlisted Sept. 20, 1861. Promoted to 2nd Lt. Co. H, Nov. 20, 1861.

Westcott, John. Promoted from Corp. Nov. 20, 1861. Mustered out Oct. 15, 1864. Died May 6, 1895. Interred at North Burial Ground, Bristol, RI.

Sergeants

Church, George H. Residence, North Kingstown. 28. M. Jeweler. Enlisted Sept. 13, 1861. KIA Mar. 14, 1862 at New Bern, NC. Interred at Elm Grove Cemetery, North Kingstown, RI.

Grinell, James S.C. Promoted from Corp. June 25, 1862. Promoted to 2nd Lt. Co. C, April 9, 1864.

Hull, George E. Promoted from Corp. WIA, shot in left thigh, July 30, 1864 at the Crater, Petersburg, VA. Mustered out Oct. 15, 1864.

Johnson, Edwin R. Residence, North Kingstown. 16. S. Laborer. Enlisted Sept. 13, 1861. Promoted to Sgt. Maj. June 29, 1862.

Morse, Benjamin E. Promoted from Corp. Promoted to 2nd Lt. Co. B, Aug. 11, 1862.

Nichols, Phillip. Promoted from Pvt. Promoted to 2nd Lt. Co. F, Jan. 13, 1863.

Nottage, Charles H. Promoted from Corp. Promoted to Commissary Sgt. and assigned to regimental staff Nov. 25, 1862.

Nottage, William M. Promoted from Corp. Trans. to Co. G, 7th R.I. Vols. Oct. 21, 1864. Mustered out July 13, 1865. Died April 9, 1916. Interred at St. Patrick's Cemetery, Providence, RI.

Reynolds, Lucien J. Promoted from Corp. May 1, 1864. WIA, shot in left thigh, July 30, 1864 at the Crater, Petersburg, VA. Mustered out Oct. 15, 1864.

Reynolds, William J. Residence, North Kingstown. 30. M. Jeweler. Enlisted Sept. 13, 1861. Promoted to 1st Lt. Co. G, Dec. 12, 1862.

Sanford, Alexander. Residence, North Kingstown. 21. S. Farmer. Enlisted Sept. 13, 1861. Died of typhoid Dec. 10, 1861 at Washington, DC. Interred at Elm Grove Cemetery, North Kingstown, RI.

Corporals

Bullock, James H. Promoted from Pvt. Jan. 1, 1863. Mustered out Oct. 15, 1864. Died 1909. Interred at Elm Grove Cemetery, North Kingstown, RI.

Burdick, William H. Residence, East Greenwich. 19. S. Clerk. Enlisted Sept. 19, 1861. Discharged for disability Nov. 30, 1862 at Philadelphia, PA. Died Feb. 8, 1907. Interred at First Cemetery, East Greenwich, RI.

Congdon, William H. Residence, North Kingstown. 33. S. Jeweler. Enlisted Sept. 13, 1861. WIA Sept. 17, 1862 at Antietam, MD. Discharged for disability Mar. 20, 1863 at Providence, RI. Interred at Elm Grove Cemetery, North Kingstown, RI.

Corey, William R. Promoted from Pvt. WIA Sept. 30, 1864 at Poplar Spring Church, VA. Mustered out Oct. 15, 1864. Died June 14, 1869. Interred at Lakewood Burial Ground, Warwick, RI.

Daken, Hugh. Promoted from Pvt. June 25, 1862. Mustered out Oct. 15, 1864.

Grinnell, James S.C. Residence, North Kingstown.28. M. Laborer. Enlisted Sept. 13, 1861. Promoted to Sgt. June 25, 1862.

Hull, George E. Promoted from Pvt. Promoted to Sgt.

Morse, Benjamin E. Residence, Providence. 25. M. Engraver. Enlisted Sept. 13, 1861. Promoted to Sgt.

Nichols, Phillip. Residence, North Kingstown. 20. S. Jeweler. Enlisted Sept. 13, 1861. Promoted to Sgt.

Nottage, Charles H. Residence, North Kingstown. 28. M. Jeweler. Enlisted Sept. 13, 1861. Promoted to Sgt.

Nottage, William M. Residence, Providence. 25. S. Seaman. Enlisted Sept. 23, 1861. Promoted to Sgt.

Reynolds, Lucien J. Promoted from Pvt. Feb. 1, 1863. Promoted to Sgt. May 1, 1864.

Seagraves, Alpheus M. Promoted from Pvt. July 30, 1864. Mustered out Oct. 15, 1864. Died Sept. 1, 1922. Interred at Prospect Hill Cemetery, Uxbridge, MA.

Thomas, George S. Promoted from Pvt. KIA July 30, 1864 at the Crater, Petersburg, VA. Cenotaph at Elm Grove Cemetery, North Kingstown, RI.

Trahay, Edward. Promoted from Pvt. Aug. 1, 1862. WIA Sept. 17, 1862 at Antietam, MD. Mustered out Oct. 15, 1864.

Westcott, John. Residence, North Kingstown. 22. M. Jeweler. Enlisted Sept. 13, 1861. Promoted to 1st Sgt. Nov. 20, 1861.

Wills, George B. Promoted from Pvt. Aug. 14, 1862. WIA, shot in arm and chest, July 30, 1864 at the Crater, Petersburg, VA. Mustered out Oct. 15, 1864. Died Dec. 1, 1927. Interred at Elm Grove Cemetery, North Kingstown, RI.

Musicians

Freeman, Henry. Residence, North Kingstown. 29. M. Laborer. Enlisted Sept. 13, 1861. Discharged for disability Sept. 29, 1862 at Baltimore, MD. Died May 22, 1900. Interred at Elm Grove Cemetery, North Kingstown, RI.

Smith, Matthew. Residence, Providence. 26. S. Musician. Enlisted Oct. 1, 1861. Trans. to Co. B, 7th R.I. Vols. Oct. 21, 1864. Mustered out July 13, 1865.

Wagoners

Bloomer, Thomas. Residence, North Kingstown. 32. S. Carpenter. Enlisted Sept. 13, 1861. Died of typhoid Oct. 11, 1864 at Alexandria, VA. Interred at Arlington National Cemetery, Arlington, VA. Section 13, Grave 13310.

Fullerton, John. Residence, Providence. 35. M. Teamster. Enlisted Sept. 23, 1861. Discharged for disability Dec. 15, 1861 at Fairfax, VA.

Privates

Abbott, Abial. J.W. Residence, Warwick. S. 16. Laborer. Enlisted Sept. 18, 1861. MWIA, shot in leg, Sept. 17, 1862 at Antietam, MD. DOW Oct. 7, 1862 near Keedysville, MD. Interred at Antietam National Cemetery, Sharpsburg, MD. Rhode Island Section, Grave 2836.

Andrews, George E. Residence, Warwick. 16. S. Laborer. Enlisted Sept. 18, 1861. Mustered out Oct. 15, 1864. Died Oct. 14, 1898. Interred at Greenwood Cemetery, Coventry, RI.

Anthony, William J. Residence, Newport. 20. S. Painter. Enlisted Aug. 14, 1862. Died of typhoid Dec. 18, 1862 at Washington, DC. Interred at Island Cemetery, Newport, RI.

Austin, Jacob V. Residence, North Kingstown. 18. S. Farmer. Enlisted Sept. 13, 1861. Died of diphtheria Sept. 1, 1863 at Portsmouth, VA. Interred at Hampton National Cemetery, Hampton, VA. Section A, Grave 3670.

Baker, Charles C. Residence, North Kingstown. 16. S. Boatman. Enlisted Sept. 13, 1861. KIA Mar. 14, 1862 at New Bern, NC. Interred at Elm Grove Cemetery, North Kingstown, RI.

Baker, Nicholas. Residence, North Kingstown. 15. S. Boatman. Enlisted Sept. 13, 1861. Mustered out Oct. 15, 1864. Died Dec. 26, 1926. Interred at Elm Grove Cemetery, North Kingstown, RI.

Barber, William. Residence, Newport. 27. M. Shoemaker. Enlisted Aug. 15, 1862. Trans. to Co. G, 7th R.I. Vols. Oct. 21, 1864.

Bassett, George. Residence, Smithfield. 18. S. Laborer. Enlisted Aug. 7, 1862. Trans. to Co. G, 7th R.I. Vols. Oct. 21, 1864. Mustered out June 9, 1865.

Bennett, Eliphalet W. Residence, North Kingstown. 24. S. Blacksmith. Enlisted Sept. 13, 1861. Mustered out Oct. 15, 1864. Died June 27, 1914. Interred at Elm Grove Cemetery, North Kingstown, RI.

Bliven, David H. Residence, Exeter. 21. S. Tailor. Enlisted Sept. 13, 1861. Discharged for disability May 31, 1862 at Beaufort, NC. Died of disease contracted in the service Aug. 9, 1864 at Exeter, RI. Interred at Wood River Cemetery, Richmond, RI.

Brownell, Wilson D. Residence, Portsmouth. 19. S. Sailor. Enlisted Sept. 18, 1861. Died of typhoid Feb. 22, 1864 at Portsmouth, RI. Interred at Portsmouth Village Cemetery, Portsmouth, RI.

Boyce, Thomas. Residence, Providence. 31. S. Laborer. Enlisted Sept. 13, 1861. Trans. to VRC Sept. 1, 1863. Died Nov. 18, 1900. Interred at Mt. Hope Cemetery, North Attleboro, MA.

Bucklin, Washington I. Residence, Providence. 18. S. Pick maker. Enlisted Sept. 18, 1861. Mustered out Oct. 15, 1864. Died 1907. Interred at North Burial Ground, Providence, RI.

Bullock, James H. Residence, North Kingstown. 18. S. Farmer. Enlisted Sept. 13, 1861. Promoted to Corp. Jan. 1, 1863.

Chapin, James T. Residence, North Kingstown. 21. S. Laborer. Enlisted Sept. 13, 1861. Discharged for disability Oct. 21, 1862 at Sharpsburg, MD. Died 1931. Interred at Elm Grove Cemetery, North Kingstown, RI.

Conley, James. Residence, Providence. 19. S. Laborer. Enlisted Oct. 1, 1861. Mustered out Oct. 15, 1864. Died April 12, 1915. Interred at North Burial Ground, Providence, RI.

Corey, William R. Residence, North Kingstown. 20. S. Boatman. Enlisted Sept. 13, 1861. Promoted to Corp.

Cozzens, John W. Residence, North Kingstown. 17. S. Boatman. Enlisted Sept. 13, 1861. Mustered out Oct. 15, 1864. Died May 5, 1897. Interred at Elm Grove Cemetery, North Kingstown, RI.

Daken, Hugh. Residence, North Kingstown. 21. S. Laborer. Enlisted Sept. 28, 1861. Promoted to Corp. June 25, 1862.

Dawley, Olney W. Residence, North Kingstown. 19. S. Farmer. Enlisted Sept. 13, 1861. Mustered out Oct. 15, 1864. Died Jan. 18, 1899. Interred at Pachaug Cemetery, Griswold, CT.

Dervine, James. Residence, North Kingstown. 24. S. Laborer. Enlisted Sept. 13, 1861. WIA, shot in groin, Sept. 17, 1862 at Antietam, MD. Mustered out Oct. 15, 1864.

Donovan, Richard. Residence, North Kingstown. 22. S. Laborer. Enlisted Sept. 13, 1861. Trans. to Co. G, 7th R.I. Vols. Oct. 21, 1864. Discharged for disability at Portsmouth Grove, RI, June 29, 1865.

Doonan, Frank. Residence, North Kingstown. 24. S. Laborer. Enlisted Sept. 23, 1861. Trans. to Co. G, 7th R.I. Vols. Oct. 21, 1864. Mustered out July 13, 1865. Interred at Calvary Catholic Cemetery, Racine, WI.

Doran, Patrick. Residence, Providence. 19. S. Clerk. Enlisted June 10, 1862. Discharged for disability June 1, 1863. Died of dysentery contracted in the service, April 29, 1865, at Providence, RI. Interred at North Burial Ground, Providence, RI.

Easterbrook, George. Residence, South Kingstown. 18. S. Farmer. Enlisted Oct. 1, 1861. CIA July 30, 1864 at the Crater, Petersburg, VA. Released and mustered out at Providence, RI, Mar. 17, 1895. Died 1930. Interred at Oak Dell Cemetery, South Kingstown, RI.

Fanning, Dennis. Residence, North Kingstown. 21. S. Laborer. Enlisted Sept. 13, 1861. Mustered out Oct. 15, 1864. Interred at Elm Grove Cemetery, North Kingstown, RI.

Flanders, Orlando D. Residence, Chelsea, MA. 21. S. Sailor. Enlisted Sept. 18, 1861. CIA July 30, 1864 at the Crater, Petersburg, VA. Trans. to Co. G, 7th R.I. Vols. Oct. 21, 1864. Mustered out July 13, 1865. Interred at Pleasant View Cemetery, Ludlow, VT.

Grant, Patrick. Residence, Providence. 20. S. Farmer. Enlisted Oct. 1, 1861. CIA July 30, 1864 at the Crater, Petersburg, VA. Released Feb. 22, 1865. Sent to U.S. Hospital, Baltimore, MD. Mustered out July 20, 1865.

Greene, Caleb. Residence, North Kingstown. 40. M. Laborer. Enlisted Sept. 13, 1861. Mustered out Oct. 15, 1864. Interred at Elm Grove Cemetery, North Kingstown, RI.

Hennessey, Thomas. Residence, Providence. 18. S. Laborer. Enlisted June 19, 1862. Discharged for disability Dec. 15, 1862 at New York, NY. Died Sept. 24, 1893. Interred at Union Cemetery, Kansas City, MO.

Higgins, James. Residence, Providence. 21. S. Clerk. Enlisted Aug. 14, 1862. Trans. to Co. G, 7th R.I. Vols. Oct. 21, 1864. Mustered out June 9, 1865.

Holden, George. Residence, Tiverton. 21. M. Dresser. Enlisted Sept. 25, 1861. WIA Mar. 14, 1862 at New Bern, NC. Mustered out Oct. 15, 1864.

Hopkins, William S. Residence, East Greenwich. 17. S. Laborer. Enlisted Sept. 13, 1861. Died of typhoid April 12, 1862 at Carolina City, NC. Interred at New Bern National Cemetery, New Bern, NC. Section 11, Grave 1878.

Hoxie, John W. Residence, East Greenwich. 33. S. Farmer. Enlisted Sept. 23, 1861. WIA, shot in left arm, July 30, 1864 at the Crater, Petersburg, VA. Trans. to Co. G, 7th R.I. Vols. Oct. 21, 1864. Mustered out July 13, 1865. Died Mar. 29, 1895. Interred at Miner Cemetery, Stonington, CT.

Hubbard, William H. Residence, Newport. Enlisted Aug. 14, 1862. Trans. to Co. G, 7th R.I. Vols. Oct. 21, 1864. Mustered out July 13, 1865.

Hull, George E. Residence, North Kingstown. 25. S. Boatman. Enlisted Sept. 13, 1861. Promoted to Corp.

Hunt, William R. Residence, North Kingstown. 21. S. Farmer. Enlisted Sept. 19, 1861. Trans. to Co. G, 7th R.I. Vols. Oct. 21, 1864. Mustered out July 13, 1865. Died July 8, 1916. Interred at Elm Grove Cemetery, North Kingstown, RI.

Lacey, Albert A. Residence, South Kingstown. 19. S. Finisher. Enlisted Sept. 13, 1861. Deserted in the face of the enemy Sept. 17, 1862 at Antietam, MD. Tried by court martial and sentenced to be executed. Sentence commuted and sentenced to hard labor. Finally released from prison and mustered out May 27, 1869.

Leach, Charles H. Residence, North Kingstown. 34. M. Operative. Enlisted Sept. 13, 1861. Deserted in the face of the enemy Sept. 17, 1862 at Antietam, MD.

McCann, Edward. Residence, Providence. 17. S. Laborer. Enlisted Sept. 19, 1861. WIA, shot in arm, Sept. 17, 1862 at Antietam, MD. Discharged for disability Dec. 16, 1862 at Baltimore, MD.

McGee, Charles. Residence, Providence. 18. S. Laborer. Enlisted Sept. 19, 1861. Discharged for disability Oct. 11, 1862.

Mitchell, Silas. Residence, New Shoreham. 22. S. Laborer. Enlisted Aug. 6, 1862. Trans. to Co. G, 7th R.I. Vols. Oct. 21, 1864. Mustered out June 9, 1865. Died Feb. 22, 1891. Interred at Knotty Oak Cemetery, Coventry, RI.

Northrup, John R. Residence, North Kingstown. 27. M. Laborer. Enlisted Sept. 13, 1861. Trans. to Co. G, 7th R.I. Vols. Oct. 21, 1864. Mustered out July 13, 1865.

Northrup, William R. Residence, North Kingstown. 19. S. Laborer. Enlisted Sept. 13, 1861. Deserted Aug. 20, 1862 at Fredericksburg, VA.

Nottage, George E. Residence, North Kingstown. 20. S. Hostler. Enlisted Sept. 23, 1861. WIA, shot in left thigh, July 30, 1864 at the Crater, Petersburg, VA. Discharged for disability Nov. 1, 1864. Died Dec. 12, 1921. Interred at Lone Fir Cemetery, Portland, OR.

Reynolds, Albert F. Residence, Providence. 22. M. Jeweler. Enlisted Sept. 23, 1861. Died of tuberculosis Dec. 3, 1862 at Portsmouth, RI. Interred at North Burial Ground, Providence, RI.

Reynolds, Lucien J. Residence, North Kingstown. 18. S. Mariner. Enlisted Sept. 18, 1861. Promoted to Corp. Feb. 1, 1863.

Richie, David. Residence, North Kingstown. 13. M. Mason. Enlisted Sept. 13, 1861. Discharged for disability May 31, 1862 at Philadelphia, PA.

Rose, Daniel R. Residence, North Kingstown. 22. S. Farmer. Enlisted Sept. 23, 1861. CIA Sept. 17, 1862 at Antietam, MD. Returned Sept. 1, 1863. Trans. to Co. G, 7th R.I. Vols. Oct. 21, 1864. Mustered out July 13, 1865. Interred at Elm Grove Cemetery, North Kingstown, RI.

Rose, Thomas G. Residence, North Kingstown. 26. M. Mason. Enlisted Sept. 13, 1861. Died of dysentery Aug. 9, 1864 at North Kingstown, RI. Interred at Elm Grove Cemetery, North Kingstown, RI.

Rumbles, Samuel A. Residence, Providence. 23. S. Laborer. Enlisted Sept. 17, 1861. Mustered out Oct. 15, 1864. Died Jan. 4, Interred at Elm Grove Cemetery, North Kingstown, RI.

Seagraves, Alpheus M. Residence, North Kingstown. 17. S. Laborer. Enlisted Sept. 13, 1861. Promoted to Corp. July 30, 1864.

Simmons, Lloyd. Residence, North Kingstown. 18. S. Farmer. Enlisted Sept. 13, 1861. Died of typhoid June 25, 1862 at Providence, RI. Interred at Swan Point Cemetery, Providence, RI.

Smith, Darius. Residence, North Kingstown. 35. S. Mariner. Enlisted Sept. 13, 1861. WIA, shot in left side, July 30, 1864 at the Crater, Petersburg, VA. Trans. to Co. G, 7th R.I. Vols. Oct. 21, 1864. Mustered out July 13, 1865. Died June 28, 1889. Interred at Elm Grove Cemetery, North Kingstown, RI.

Smith, John W. Residence, North Kingstown. 27. M. Mariner. Enlisted Sept. 13, 1861. Mustered out Oct. 15, 1864. Died 1888. Interred at Elm Grove Cemetery, North Kingstown, RI.

Smith, Thomas A. Residence, North Kingstown. 15. S. Laborer. Enlisted Sept. 13, 1861. Trans. to Co. G, 7th RI Vols. Oct. 21, 1864. Mustered out July 13, 1865. Died May 7, 1911. Interred at Elm Grove Cemetery, North Kingstown, RI.

Sweet, Samuel C. Residence, North Kingstown. 23. M. Jeweler. Enlisted Sept. 13, 1861. Discharged for disability Jan. 31, 1863 at Providence, RI. Died Mar. 6, 1909. Interred at Elm Grove Cemetery, North Kingstown, RI.

Taplin, William. Residence, New Shoreham. 42. M. Shoe maker. Enlisted Sept. 18, 1861. Discharged for disability Jan. 20, 1863. Died Aug. 7, 1898. Interred at First Cemetery, East Greenwich, RI.

Taylor, Edward E. Residence, Newport. 30. M. Fisherman. Enlisted Aug. 14, 1862. WIA, shot in foot, Sept. 17, 1862 at Antietam, MD. Trans. to Co. G, 7th R.I. Vols. Oct. 21, 1864. Mustered out June 9, 1865. Died April 12, 1866. Interred at Common Burial Ground, Newport, RI.

Tillinghast, Benjamin R. Residence, North Kingstown. 33. M. Machinist. Enlisted Sept. 13, 1861. Mustered out Oct. 15, 1864. Died 1873. Interred at Elm Grove Cemetery, North Kingstown, RI.

Thomas, George S. Residence, North Kingstown. 21. S. Farmer. Enlisted Sept. 5, 1861. Promoted to Corp.

Tourgee, John F. Residence, North Kingstown. 20. M. Operative. Enlisted Sept. 13, 1861. Died of dysentery Nov. 23, 1862 at Washington, DC. Interred at Elm Grove Cemetery, North Kingstown, RI.

Tourgee, Thomas H. Residence, North Kingstown. 23. M. Teamster. Enlisted Sept. 13, 1861. Mustered out Oct. 15, 1864. Died Mar. 15, 1909. Interred at Elm Grove Cemetery, North Kingstown, RI.

Trahay, Edward. Residence, Newport. 19. S. Laborer. Enlisted Sept. 13, 1861. Promoted to Corp. Aug. 1, 1862.
Trumbull, John A. Residence, Warwick. 24. S. Laborer. Enlisted Sept. 23, 1861. WIA, shot in right hand, July 30, 1864 at the Crater, Petersburg, VA. Mustered out Oct. 15, 1864.

Trimm, George W. Residence, Providence. 24. M. Operative. Enlisted Sept. 19, 1861. Discharged for disability May 5, 1863 at Providence, RI. Died November 27, 1881. Interred at Slatersville Cemetery, North Smithfield, RI.

Troutz, George. Residence, Providence. 30. S. Jeweler. Enlisted Sept. 20, 1861. Trans. to Co. G, 7th R.I. Vols. Oct. 21, 1864. Mustered out July 13, 1865.

Tully, Mark. Residence, North Kingstown. 33. M. Jeweler. Enlisted Sept. 13, 1861. Mustered out Oct. 15, 1864. Died Dec. 16, 1902. Interred at Oak Hill Cemetery, Pownal, VT.

Whaland, Bernard. Residence, North Kingstown. 22. S. Laborer. Enlisted Sept. 13, 1861. Mustered out Oct. 15, 1864. Interred at St. Patrick's Cemetery, East Greenwich, RI.

Westcott, John. Residence, North Kingstown. 18. S. Jeweler. Enlisted Sept. 13, 1861. Promoted to Corp. June 25, 1862.

Whipple, William D. Residence, Providence. 18. S. Carpenter. Enlisted Aug. 15, 1862. Trans. to Co. G, 7th R.I. Vols. Oct. 21, 1864. Mustered out June 9, 1865. Interred at Benedict Whipple Lot, Scituate Cemetery 78, Scituate, RI.

Willis, Frederick. Residence, North Kingstown. 19. S. Laborer. Enlisted Sept. 18, 1861. Discharged for disability Jan. 10, 1863 at Providence, RI.

Willis, George B. Residence, North Kingstown. 23. M. Jeweler. Enlisted Sept. 13, 1861. Promoted to Corp. Aug. 14, 1862.

Willis, Jeremiah. Residence, North Kingstown. 19. S. Laborer. Enlisted Sept. 18, 1861. Trans. to Co. G, 7th R.I. Vols. Oct. 21, 1864. Mustered out July 13, 1865. Died Jan. 6, 1910. Interred at Elm Grove Cemetery, North Kingstown, RI.

Willis, Layton B. Residence, North Kingstown. 21. S. Farmer. Enlisted Sept. 18, 1861. WIA, shot in leg, Sept. 17, 1861 at Antietam, MD. Discharged for disability Mar. 11, 1863 at Frederick, MD. Died Jan. 7, 1902. Interred at Elm Grove Cemetery, North Kingstown, RI.

Wilson, William. Residence, Providence. 29. S. Farmer. Enlisted Sept. 20, 1861. Mustered out Oct. 15, 1864.

COMPANY I

Captains

Bowen, Caleb T. Promoted from 1st Lt. Co. H, Aug. 11, 1862. WIA and CIA Sept. 17, 1862 at Antietam, MD. Released July 1863. Trans. to Co. G, Aug. 13, 1863.

Brown, Edward P. Promoted from 1st Lt. Co. I, Mar. 2, 1863. On brigade staff for most of 1864. Trans. to Co. D, 7th R.I. Vols. Oct. 21, 1864. Brevet major for heroism at storming of Petersburg, April 2, 1865. Resigned June 5, 1865. Died July 26, 1909. Interred at Woodlawn Cemetery, Bronx, NY.

Lapham, Erastus E. Promoted from 1st Lt. Co. I, Nov. 20, 1861. Resigned Aug. 11, 1862. Died Dec. 10, 1891. Interred at Elmwood Cemetery, Centralia, IL.

First Lieutenants

Brown, Edward P. Promoted from 2nd Lt. Co. I, Jan. 13, 1863. Promoted to Capt. Co. I, Mar. 2, 1863.

Lapham, Erastus E. Residence, Providence. Commissioned Sept. 24, 1861. Promoted to Capt. Co. I, Nov. 20, 1861.

Nichols, Phillip. Promoted from 2nd Lt. Co. I, Mar. 26, 1864. Mustered out Oct. 15, 1864.

Second Lieutenants

Brown, Edward P. Residence, Rehoboth, MA. Commissioned Aug. 27, 1862. Promoted to 1st Lt. Co. I, Jan. 13, 1863.

Johnson, Charles H. Residence, Providence. Commissioned Oct. 1, 1861. Promoted to 1st Lt. Co. A, Nov. 20, 1861.

Nichols, Phillip. Promoted from Sgt. Co. H. Jan. 13, 1863. Promoted to 1st Lt. Co. I, Mar. 26, 1864.

Smith, Zerah B. Promoted from Q.M. Sgt. Nov. 20, 1861. Resigned Feb. 24, 1862. Died Dec. 29, 1898. Interred at Swan Point Cemetery, Providence, RI.

First Sergeants

Moies, John E. Residence, Smithfield. 26. S. Salesman. Enlisted Sept. 24, 1861. WIA Sept. 17, 1862 at Antietam, MD. Promoted to 1st Lt. USCT. Nov. 1, 1863. Died Oct. 19, 1865. Interred at Mineral Spring Cemetery, Pawtucket, RI.

Sholes, Albert E. Promoted from Sgt. Nov. 1, 1863. Mustered out Oct. 15, 1864. Died July 29, 1931. Interred at Vale Cemetery, Schenectady, NY.

Sergeants

Barber, Thomas A. Promoted from Pvt. Mustered out Oct. 15, 1864. Died Sept. 27, 1918. Interred at Oak Grove Cemetery, Hopkinton, RI.

Crowningshield, John A. Residence, Cumberland. 29. M. Operative. Enlisted Sept. 14, 1861. Trans. to VRC July 16, 1863. Interred at Moshassuck Cemetery, Central Falls, RI.

Crowningshield, George F. Residence, Cumberland. 31. S. Jeweler. Enlisted Oct. 1, 1861. Promoted to 2nd Lt. Co. E, Nov. 20, 1861.

Eggleston, John B. Promoted from Pvt. Mustered out Oct. 15, 1864. Died Mar. 4, 1899. Interred at Hillside Cemetery, Townsend, MA.

Farnum, Samuel W. Promoted from Pvt. Mustered out Oct. 15, 1864. Died Mar. 24, 1890. Interred at Noah Farnum Lot, Smithfield Cemetery 102, Smithfield, RI.

Martin, Edward. Promoted from Corp. Mustered out Oct. 15,1864. Died July 10, 1906. Interred at Brayton Cemetery, Warwick, RI.

Olney, William C. Residence, Pawtucket. 21. S. Carpenter. Enlisted Sept. 14, 1861. Promoted to 2nd Lt. Co. G, Jan. 12, 1863.

Sholes, Albert E. Residence, Cumberland. 18. S. Student. Enlisted Sept. 20, 1861. Promoted to 1st Sgt. Nov. 1, 1863.

Taylor, William. Promoted from Corp. April 11, 1862. Discharged for disability Feb. 4, 1863 at Alexandria, VA.

Wilson, James. Promoted from Corp. April 11, 1862. Discharged for disability Sept. 27, 1862 at Providence, RI. Interred at Riverside Cemetery, Pawtucket, RI.

Corporals

Collins, Matthew. Promoted from Pvt. Mustered out Oct. 15, 1864.

Guiot, Joseph. Promoted from Pvt. WIA, shot in thumb, Sept. 17, 1862 at Antietam, MD. Mustered out Oct. 15, 1864.

Hayes, John. Promoted from Pvt. KIA Sept. 17, 1862 at Antietam, MD.

Hopkins, Henry V. Promoted from Pvt. MWIA Sept. 17, 1862 at Antietam, MD. DOW Oct. 26, 1862 at Sharpsburg, MD. Interred at Oak Grove Cemetery, Pawtucket, RI.

Lewis, Benoni. Promoted from Pvt. Mustered out Oct. 15, 1864. Died Nov. 23, 1914. Interred at Pocasset Cemetery, Cranston, RI.

Lincoln, Henry D. Residence, Pawtucket. 22. S. Moulder. Enlisted Sept. 14, 1861. WIA, shot in hand, Sept. 17, 1862 at Antietam, MD. WIA, shot in left arm, July 30, 1864 at the Crater, Petersburg, VA. Mustered out Oct. 15, 1864. Died May 22, 1900. Interred at Woodlawn Cemetery, Attleboro, MA.

Mahan, Thomas. Residence, Pawtucket. 22. S. Operative. Enlisted Sept. 14, 1861. Trans. to Regular Army Oct. 30, 1862.

Martin, Edward. Residence, Warwick. 21. S. Operative. Enlisted Sept. 13, 1861. Promoted to Sgt.

Murray, James. Residence, Providence. 22. S. Laborer. Enlisted Sept. 27, 1861. Deserted Jan. 26, 1863 at Falmouth, VA.

Rhodes, Charles F. Residence, Providence. 33. S. Machinist. Enlisted Sept. 28, 1861. Mustered out Oct. 15, 1864.

Shepley, John. Promoted from Pvt. Trans. to Co. D, 7th R.I. Vols. Oct. 21, 1864. Mustered out June 9, 1865. Died Nov. 13, 1903. Interred at Swan Point Cemetery, Providence, RI.

Stanley, William H. Promoted from Pvt. Served as adjutant's clerk. Mustered out Oct. 15, 1864.

Taylor, William. Promoted from Pvt. Promoted to Sgt. April 11, 1862.

Wilson, James. Residence, Pawtucket. 24. S. Moulder. Enlisted Sept. 14, 1861. WIA Mar. 14, 1862 at New Bern, NC. Promoted to Sgt. April 11, 1862.

Musicians

Longstreet, Frank. Residence, Providence. 17. S. Clerk. Enlisted May 9, 1862. Trans. to Co. D, 7th R.I. Vols. Oct. 21, 1864. Mustered out May 13, 1865.

Otis, Morris. Residence, Cumberland. 26. M. Operative. Enlisted Sept. 24, 1861. Trans. to Regular Army Oct. 30, 1862.

Sexton, Bartholomew. Residence, Cumberland. 21. S. Operative. Enlisted Sept. 14, 1861. Mustered out Oct. 15, 1864. Died 1895. Interred at Old St. Mary's Cemetery, Pawtucket, RI.

Wagoner

Morris, Lyman. Residence, Cumberland. 45. M. Operative. Enlisted Sept. 14, 1861. Mustered out Oct. 15, 1864. Interred at Cumberland Cemetery, Cumberland, RI.

Privates

Ashton, William J. Residence, Providence. 36. M. Weaver. Enlisted Sept. 21, 1861. Mustered out Oct. 25, 1864. Died Sept. 19, 1903. Interred at North Burial Ground, Providence, RI.

Armstrong, John. Residence, Providence. 19. S. Laborer. Enlisted Sept. 16, 1864. Trans. to Co. D, 7th R.I. Vols. Oct. 21, 1864. Mustered out July 13, 1865. Died Sept. 10, 1897. Interred at St. Mary's Cemetery, New Bedford, MA.

Barber, Thomas A. Residence, Hopkinton. 21. S. Farmer. Enlisted Sept. 14, 1861. Promoted to Sgt.

Barrington, John. Residence, Pawtucket. 37. M. Laborer. Enlisted Sept. 28, 1861. Mustered out Oct. 15, 1864.

Bethel, Richard. Residence, Concord, NH. 21. S. Farmer. Enlisted Sept. 21, 1861. Mustered out Oct. 15, 1864. Died 1888. Interred Oak Grove Cemetery, Pawtucket, RI.

Briggs, Charles H. Residence, Uxbridge, MA. 18. S. Operative. Enlisted Sept. 24, 1861. Died of typhoid at Carolina City, NC, April 24, 1862. Interred at New Bern National Cemetery, New Bern, NC. Section 11, Grave 1874.

Brown, Abial. Residence, Cumberland. 21. S. Hostler. Enlisted Sept. 14, 1861. Discharged for disability Feb. 17, 1863 at Alexandria, VA. Died Mar. 24, 1899. Interred at Spring Grove Cemetery, Hartford, CT.

Brown, Emanuel. Residence, Cumberland. 23. S. Carpenter. Enlisted Sept. 28, 1861. WIA, shot in head, July 30, 1864, at the Crater, Petersburg, VA. Mustered out Oct. 15, 1864.

Brown, William. Residence, Providence. 21. S. Laborer. Enlisted Sept. 24, 1861. Discharged for disability Feb. 14, 1863 at Washington, DC.

Brownell, Daniel W. Residence, Warwick. 24. S. Wool sorter. Enlisted Sept. 21, 1861. Discharged for disability Sept. 20, 1862 at Beaufort, NC.

Campbell, Bernard. Residence, Warwick. 18. S. Painter. Enlisted Sept. 20, 1861. WIA, left arm amputated, Sept. 17, 1862 at Antietam, MD. Discharged for disability Dec. 1, 1862 at Baltimore, MD. Died Nov. 27, 1909. Interred at St. Mary's Cemetery, West Warwick, RI.

Carpenter, Joseph B. Residence, Pawtucket. 21. S. Farmer. Enlisted Sept. 19, 1861. Mustered out Oct. 15, 1864. Died 1908. Interred at Carpenter Cemetery, North Attleboro, MA.

Coffey, Peter. Residence, Providence. 18. S. Laborer. Enlisted Mar. 11, 1864. Trans. to Co. D, 7th R.I. Vols. Oct. 21, 1864. Mustered out July 13, 1865.

Collins, Matthew. Residence, Cumberland. 21. S. Operative. Enlisted Sept. 14, 1861. Promoted to Corp.

Coyle, Hugh. Residence, Taunton, MA. 27. S. Mason. Enlisted Aug. 15, 1862. Mustered out Oct. 15, 1864.

Crocker, George F. Residence, Attleboro, MA. 21. S. Butcher. Enlisted Sept. 19, 1861. Mustered out Oct. 15, 1864. Died May 16, 1915. Interred at Moshassuck Cemetery, Central Falls, RI.

Crosby, Samuel. Residence, Warwick. 38. M. Laborer. Enlisted Sept. 24, 1861. Discharged for disability Oct. 28, 1862.

Duffy, John. Residence, Warwick. 22. S. Painter. Enlisted Sept. 20, 1861. WIA, shot in arm, Sept. 17, 1862 at Antietam, MD. Trans. to VRC Sept. 1, 1863. Interred at St. Ann's Cemetery, Cranston, RI.

Earle, Tyler B. Residence, Woonsocket. 34. M. Operator. Enlisted Aug. 20, 1862. Mustered out Oct. 15, 1864. Interred at Glenford Cemetery, Scituate, RI.

Eston, Elisha. Residence, Providence. 42. M. Machinist. Enlisted Sept. 24, 1861. Discharged for disability Jan. 23, 1863 at New York, NY.

Eggleston, John B. Residence, Cumberland. 16. S. Farmer. Enlisted Sept. 28, 1861. Promoted to Sgt.

Farnum, Samuel W. Residence, Smithfield.23. S. Cigar maker. Enlisted Sept. 14, 1861. Promoted to Sgt.

Farrell, William. Residence, Pawtucket. 21. S. Operator. Enlisted Sept. 21, 1861. Trans. to Regular Army Oct. 24, 1862. Died Aug. 24, 1917. Interred at St. Mary's Cemetery, West Warwick, RI.

Fuller, Charles H. Residence, Pawtucket. 23. M. Farmer. Enlisted Sept. 14, 1861. Mustered out Oct. 15, 1864. Interred at Riverside Cemetery, Pawtucket, RI.

Gorton, Samuel H. Residence, Cumberland. 19. S. Farmer. Enlisted Sept. 26, 1861. Mustered out Oct. 15, 1864.

Greene, Daniel H. Residence, Providence. 19. S. Student. Enlisted Sept. 19, 1861. CIA July 30, 1864 at the Crater, Petersburg, VA. Trans. to Co. D, 7th R.I. Vols. Oct. 21, 1864. Mustered out July 21, 1865. Died Mar. 11, 1911. Interred at North Burial Ground, Providence, RI.

Griswold, Edward. Residence, Pawtucket. 44. M. Farmer. Enlisted Sept, 28, 1861. Discharged for disability Feb. 14, 1863 at Alexandria, VA.

Guiot, Joseph. Residence, Cumberland. 24. M. Operative. Enlisted Sept. 24, 1861. Promoted to Corp.

Hayes, John. Residence, Tiverton. 19. S. Laborer. Enlisted Sept. 24, 1861. Promoted to Corp.

Healey, Luke. Residence, Woonsocket. 19. S. Box maker. Enlisted Sept. 24, 1861. Mustered out Oct. 15, 1864. Died May 22, 1889. Interred at Intervale Cemetery, North Providence, RI.

Hill, George B. Residence, Exeter. 42. M. Operative. Enlisted Sept. 14, 1861. Discharged for disability Feb. 28, 1863 at Washington, DC. Interred at Moshassuck Cemetery, Central Falls, RI.

Hill, Reuben. Residence, Exeter. 38. M. Machinist. Enlisted Sept. 25, 1861. Discharged for disability June 3, 1862 at Philadelphia, PA. Interred at Moshassuck Cemetery, Central Falls, RI.

Holbrook, John. Residence, Douglas, MA. 35. M. Farmer. Enlisted Sept. 14, 1861. Discharged for disability Nov. 20, 1862 at Alexandria, VA.

Hopkins, Adin B. Residence, Blackstone, MA. 18. S. Farmer. Enlisted Sept. 19, 1861. KIA Mar. 14, 1862 at New Bern, NC. Interred at Oak Grove Cemetery, Pawtucket, RI.

Hopkins, Henry V. Residence, Warwick. 19. S. Operative. Enlisted Sept. 24, 1861. Promoted to Corp.

Hughes, John. Residence, Warwick. 21. S. Operative. Enlisted Sept. 14, 1861. Mustered out Oct. 15, 1864. Interred at St. Patrick's Cemetery, East Greenwich, RI.

Hunt, Daniel D. Residence, North Kingstown. 19. S. Farmer. Enlisted Mar. 11, 1864. Trans. to Co. D, 7th R.I. Vols. Oct. 21, 1864. Mustered out at Washington, DC, July 5, 1865. Died Dec. 7, 1898. Interred at Rufus-Hunt Cemetery, North Kingstown Cemetery 10, North Kingstown, RI.

Hunt, Leonard A. Residence, North Kingstown. 18. S. Farmer. Enlisted April 11, 1864. CIA July 30, 1864 at the Crater, Petersburg, VA. Trans. to Co. D, 7th R.I. Vols. Oct. 21, 1864. Mustered out July 13, 1865. Interred at Mt. Hope Cemetery, Swansea, MA.

Kearn, Thomas. Residence, Norwich, CT. 19. S. Farmer. Enlisted Sept. 24, 1861. WIA Sept. 17, 1862 at Antietam, MD. Trans. to VRC Oct. 15, 1863.

Kettle, Charles. Residence, Coventry. 33. S. Spinner. Enlisted Aug. 6, 1862. CIA July 30, 1864 at the Crater, Petersburg, VA. Trans. to Co. D, 7th R.I. Vols. Oct. 21, 1864. Died of dysentery in hospital at Camp Parole, Annapolis, MD, Mar. 19, 1865. Interred at Annapolis National Cemetery, Annapolis, MD. Section C, Grave 1068.

Lawton, Benjamin F. Residence, Warwick. 36. S. Operative. Enlisted Sept. 24, 1861. Mustered out Oct. 15, 1864. Died Oct. 22, 1894. Interred at Common Burial Ground, Newport, RI.

Lewis, Benoni. Residence, Warwick. 19. S. Seaman. Enlisted Sept. 24, 1861. Promoted to Corp.

Lynch, Edward A. Residence, Providence. 37. M. Laborer. Enlisted Sept. 21, 1861. KIA Sept. 17, 1862 at Antietam, MD.

Lynch, Patrick. Residence, Providence. 21. S. Needle maker. Enlisted Sept. 24, 1861. Mustered out Oct. 15, 1864. Interred at St. Francis Cemetery, Pawtucket, RI.

McCandless, Robert. Residence, Pawtucket. 30. M. Bleacher. Enlisted Sept. 14, 1861. KIA Sept. 17, 1862 at Antietam, MD.

McGill, John. Residence, Providence. 25. M. Laborer. Enlisted Mar. 9, 1864. Trans. to Co. D, 7th R.I. Vols. Oct. 21, 1864. Discharged for disability June 10, 1865.

McGregor, Henry. Residence, Newport. 27. S. Mason. Enlisted Sept. 21, 1861. Deserted Jan. 20, 1863 at Falmouth, VA.

Maroney, Matthew. Residence, Warwick. 25. S. Mason. Enlisted Sept. 20, 1861. WIA, shot in arm, Sept. 17, 1862 at Antietam, MD. Discharged for disability May 25, 1863 at Alexandria, VA.

Martin, William. Residence, Providence. 25. M. Laborer. Enlisted Sept. 21, 1861. Discharged for disability April 30, 1863 at Alexandria, VA.

Matthewson, Thomas. Residence, Cumberland. 21. S. Farmer. Enlisted Sept. 19, 1861. Mustered out Oct. 15, 1864. Died 1914. Interred at Knotty Oak Cemetery, Coventry, RI.

Moore, Joseph B. Residence, Smithfield. 37. S. Laborer. Enlisted Aug. 12, 1862. MWIA Sept. 17, 1862 at Antietam, MD. DOW Jan. 10, 1863 at Alexandria, VA.

Morse, Willard. Residence, Uxbridge, MA. 21. S. Shoe maker. Enlisted Sept. 24, 1861. Mustered out Oct. 15, 1864.

Murphy, Cornelius. Residence, Providence. 18. S. Laborer. Enlisted Sept. 21, 1861. Died of dysentery Sept. 23, 1864 at Providence, RI. Interred at North Burial Ground, Providence, RI.

Murphy, Edward. Residence, Providence. 38. M. Sailor. Enlisted Sept. 24, 1861. Discharged for disability Feb. 28, 1863 at Alexandria, VA. Died Nov. 22, 1888. Interred at Togus National Cemetery, Augusta, ME. Grave 692.

Neagle, David. Residence, Warwick. 33. M. Laborer. Enlisted Sept. 20, 1861. Discharged for disability Sept. 20, 1862 at Beaufort, NC.

Newell, Charles A. Residence, Cumberland. 18. S. Farmer. Enlisted Sept. 19, 1861. Trans. to Regular Army Oct. 25, 1862.

Newman, Nelson T. Residence, Pawtucket. 26. S. Carpenter. Enlisted Sept. 24, 1861. Mustered out Oct. 15, 1864.

Northrup, Libbeus. Residence, North Providence. 42. M. Carpenter. Enlisted Sept. 14, 1861. Trans. to VRC Sept. 30, 1863.

Quinn, John. Residence, Providence. 25. S. Laborer. Enlisted Sept. 24, 1861. Trans. to Co. D, 7th R.I. Vols. Oct. 21, 1864. Mustered out July 13, 1865.

Patt, Benjamin A. Residence, Cumberland. 18. S. Farmer. Enlisted Sept. 14, 1861. WIA Sept. 17, 1862 at Antietam, MD. Mustered out Oct. 15, 1864. Died Mar. 19, 1909. Interred at Oak Grove Cemetery, Providence, RI.

Phetteplace, David. Residence, Smithfield. 41. S. Boot maker. Enlisted Sept. 28, 1861. Deserted Jan. 26, 1863 at Falmouth, VA. Died April 7, 1907. Interred at North Burial Ground, Bristol, RI.

Phetteplace, Otis. Residence, North Kingstown. 26. M. Laborer. Enlisted Sept. 28, 1861. Discharged for disability Aug. 8, 1862 at Fredericksburg, VA. Died Dec. 29, 1900. Interred at Cedar Cemetery, Jamestown, RI.

Remington, Andrew J. Residence, Scituate. 18. S. Laborer. Enlisted Sept. 28, 1861. Died of small pox Mar. 5, 1862 at

Washington, DC. Interred at Soldier's Home National Cemetery, Washington, DC. Section G, Grave 826.

Riley, Peter. Residence, Providence. 18. S. Laborer. Enlisted Aug. 7, 1862. Trans. to Co. D, 7th R.I. Vols. Oct. 21, 1864. Mustered out June 9, 1865.

Sherman, Edward. Residence, Newport. 18. S. Laborer. Enlisted Aug. 9, 1862. Died of typhoid Dec. 6, 1862 at Falmouth, VA.

Shepley, John. Residence, Newport. 19. S. Laborer. Enlisted Aug. 7, 1862. Promoted to Corp.

Springer, George. Residence, Newport. 23. M. Brush maker. Enlisted Sept. 24, 1861. Discharged for disability May 31, 1862 at Beaufort, NC. Interred at Pocasset Hill Cemetery, Tiverton, RI.

Stanley, William H. Residence, Warwick. 23. S. Seaman. Enlisted Sept. 24, 1861. Promoted to Corp.

Stillman, Horace. Residence, Hopkinton. 22. S. Farmer. Enlisted Sept. 20, 1861. Discharged for disability June 1, 1864 at Portsmouth, RI. Died 1911. Interred at First Cemetery, Hopkinton, RI.

Sunderland, William N. Residence, Warwick. 21. M. Baker. Enlisted Sept. 21, 1861. Trans. to Co. D, 7th R.I. Vols. Oct. 21, 1864. Mustered out July 13, 1865. Died May 2, 1896. Interred at Togus National Cemetery, Augusta, ME. Grave 1269.

Taylor, William. Residence, Cumberland. 29. M. Moulder. Enlisted Sept. 14, 1861. Promoted to Corp.

Thomas, Elisha. Residence, Cranston. 44. M. Farmer. Enlisted Aug. 28, 1862. Trans. to Co. D, 7th R.I. Vols. Oct. 21, 1864. Mustered out June 9, 1865.

Verry, Elijah. Residence, North Kingstown. 45. M . Stone cutter. Enlisted Sept. 24, 1861. Mustered out Oct. 15, 1864.

Wallahan, John. Residence, Providence. 27. M. File cutter. Enlisted Sept. 21, 1861. Discharged for disability Nov. 24, 1862 at Alexandria, VA.

Waters, Edward. Residence, Tiverton. 18. S. Laborer. Enlisted Sept. 24, 1861. WIA, shot in arm, Sept. 17, 1862 at Antietam, MD. Discharged for disability Dec. 1, 1862.

Whaylin, James. Residence, Warwick. 38. M. Laborer. Enlisted Sept. 23, 1861. Discharged for disability Sept. 26, 1862 at Beaufort, NC.

Winterbottom, John. Residence, Providence. 23. M. File cutter. Enlisted Sept. 21, 1861. WIA Sept. 17, 1862 at Antietam, MD. Mustered out Oct. 15, 1864. Remained in hospital at Washington, DC, and DOW May 5, 1865. Interred at St. Elizabeth's Hospital West Cemetery, Washington, DC.

Whipple, Charles H. Residence, Cumberland. 16. S. Farmer. Enlisted Sept. 28, 1861. Mustered out Oct. 15, 1864. Died Mar. 19, 1900. Interred at Union Village Cemetery, North Smithfield, RI.

Wood, George. Residence, Pawtucket. 44. M. Engraver. Enlisted Sept. 24, 1861. CIA Sept. 17, 1862 at Antietam, MD. Returned to regiment. Mustered out Oct. 15, 1864.

Woodward, Nathan B. Residence, Warwick. 32. M. Operator. Enlisted Sept. 23, 1861. Discharged for disability Oct. 23, 1862 at Baltimore, MD. Died Oct. 11, 1902. Interred at Riverside Cemetery, Sterling, CT.

COMPANY K

Captains

Chase, Frank A. Promoted from 1st Lt. Co. K, Aug. 11, 1862. WIA July 25, 1864 at Petersburg, VA. Mustered out Oct. 15, 1864. Interred at Swan Point Cemetery, Providence, RI.

Wood, William C. Promoted from 1st Lt. Co. K, Nov. 20, 1861. Resigned Aug. 11, 1862. Died 1916. Interred at Arlington National Cemetery, Arlington, VA. Section 2, Grave 3631.

First Lieutenants

Chase, Frank A. Promoted from 2nd Lt. Co. K, Nov. 20, 1861. Promoted to Capt. Co. K, Aug. 11, 1862.

Crowningshield, George F. Promoted from 2nd Lt. Co. E, Aug. 11, 1862. On brigade staff until mustered out Oct. 15, 1864. Died 1884. Interred at Moshassuck Cemetery, Central Falls, RI.

Wood, William C. Residence, Providence. Commissioned Oct. 30, 1861. Promoted to Capt. Co. K, Nov. 20, 1861.

Second Lieutenants

Chase, Frank A. Residence, Providence. Commissioned Oct. 2, 1861. Promoted to 1st Lt. Co. K, Nov. 20, 1861.

Eldridge, Charles E. Residence, Providence. Promoted from Sgt. Battery C, First R.I. Light Artillery Jan. 23, 1863. WIA, shot in shoulder, July 30, 1864 at the Crater, Petersburg, VA. Mustered out Oct. 15, 1864.

Hunt, Charles H. Promoted from Sgt. Co. F, Aug. 11, 1862. Resigned Feb. 1, 1863. Died July 18, 1910. Interred at Portland Memorial Mausoleum, Portland, OR.

Starkweather, Henry L. Promoted from Sgt. Co. D, Nov. 20, 1861. Resigned Aug. 11, 1862. Died Feb. 8, 1914. Interred at Los Angeles National Cemetery, Los Angeles, CA. Section 24, Row E, Grave 9.

First Sergeants

Burdick, Albert N. Promoted from Corp. Co. G, Dec. 8, 1861. Promoted to 2nd Lt. Co. B, Dec. 8, 1861.

Gorton, Charles A. Promoted from Sgt. Dec. 8, 1861. MWIA July 30, 1864 at the Crater, Petersburg, VA. DOW as a POW Dec. 6, 1864 at Salisbury, NC. Interred in mass grave at Salisbury National Cemetery, Salisbury, NC.

Sergeants

Baker, William C. Promoted from Corp. Dec. 12, 1861. WIA, shot in thigh, July 30, 1864 at the Crater, Petersburg, VA. Mustered out Oct. 15, 1864. Interred at Oakland Cemetery, Cranston, RI.

Burbank, James H. Promoted from Pvt. Oct. 23, 1862. Trans. to Co. B, 7th R.I. Vols. Oct. 21, 1864. Medal of Honor Recipient for heroism at Black Water, VA. Mustered out July 13, 1865. Died Feb. 15, 1911. Interred at Miltonvale Cemetery, Miltonvale, KS.

Fish, Stephen F. Residence, Bristol. 30. M. Clerk. Enlisted Sept. 25, 1861. Discharged for disability Dec. 6, 1863 at Frederick, MD. Died of disease contracted in the service June 4, 1866 at Bristol, RI. Interred at Portsmouth Cemetery, Portsmouth, RI.

Gladding, John A. C. Residence, Bristol. 35. M. Seaman. Enlisted Sept. 25, 1861. Discharged for disability Nov. 3, 1862. Died June 27, 1905. Interred at Juniper Hill Cemetery, Bristol, RI.

Gorton, Charles A. Promoted from Corp. Oct. 1, 1861. Promoted to 1st Sgt. Dec. 8, 1861.

Thornton, Richard H. Residence, Warwick. 22. S. Boatman. Enlisted Sept. 23, 1861. WIA, left leg amputated, July 30, 1864 at the Crater, Petersburg, VA. Discharged for disability Jan. 25, 1865 at Washington, DC. Died 1922. Interred at Pawtuxet Burial Yard, Warwick, RI.

Corporals

Baker, William C. Residence, Providence. 27. M. Boatsman. Enlisted Sept. 25, 1861. Promoted to Sgt. Dec. 12, 1861.

Burrill, Leroy. Promoted from Pvt. Trans to Co. B, 7th R.I. Vols. Oct. 21, 1864. Mustered out July 13, 1865. Died June 14, 1896. Interred at South Easton Cemetery, Easton, MA.

Coggeshall, Thomas J. Promoted from Pvt. CIA July 30, 1864 at the Crater, Petersburg, VA. Trans. to Co. B, 7th R.I. Vols. Oct. 21, 1864.

Gifford, Henry C. Promoted from Pvt. Dec. 12, 1861. Discharged for disability Sept. 8, 1862 at Beaufort, NC.

Gladding, Henry F. Promoted from Pvt. Died of dysentery May 7, 1864 at Portsmouth, RI. Interred at North Burial Ground, Bristol, RI.

Gorton, Charles A. Promoted from Pvt. Promoted to Sgt. Oct. 1, 1861.

Mott, Allen B. Residence, Warwick. 33. M. Painter. Enlisted Sept. 23, 1861. Served as 9th Corps Postmaster. Mustered out Oct. 15,

1864. Died Feb. 28, 1892. Interred at Pawtuxet Memorial Cemetery, Warwick, RI.

Shumway, Charles E. Promoted from Pvt. July 30, 1864. Died Feb. 10, 1917. Interred at Danville National Cemetery, Danville, IL. Section 9, Grave 2415.

Sweet, Ferdinand. Promoted from Pvt. Dec. 12, 1861. WIA, shot in arm, Sept. 17, 1862 at Antietam, MD. Discharged for disability Dec. 26, 1862 at Providence, RI. Died Sept. 19, 1898. Interred at Mineral Spring Cemetery, Pawtucket, RI.

Musician

Clarke, William H. Residence, Providence. 15. S. Student. Enlisted Oct. 4, 1861. Discharged for disability Aug. 25, 1862 at Fredericksburg, VA.

Privates

Adams, John H. Residence, Bristol. 20. S. Farmer. Enlisted Sept. 30, 1861. Mustered out Oct. 15, 1864.

Arnold, Oliver G. Residence, Warwick. 21. S. Trader. Enlisted Sept. 25, 1861. Mustered out Oct. 15, 1864. Died Jan. 3, 1883. Interred at Riverside Cemetery, South Kingstown, RI.

Ballou, George E. Residence, Warwick. 27. M. Farmer. Enlisted Sept. 23, 1861. Trans. to Co. B, 7th R.I. Vols. Oct. 21, 1864. Died of typhoid at Lincoln Hospital, Washington, DC, Jan. 27, 1865. Interred at Arlington National Cemetery, Arlington, VA. Section 13, Grave 9396.

Bartlett, Emor H. Residence, Smithfield. 26. M. Farmer. Enlisted Sept. 17, 1861. Discharged for disability Mar. 17, 1863 at Providence, RI.

Blake, James. Residence, Providence. 37. M. Gardiner. Enlisted Sept. 20, 1861. Trans. to Co. B, 7th R.I. Vols. Oct. 21, 1864.

Mustered out July 13, 1865. Died 1900. Interred at Pascoag Cemetery, Burrillville, RI.

Bligh, John. Residence, Coventry. 17. S. Weaver. Enlisted Sept. 30, 1861. Trans. to Co. B, 7th R.I. Vols. Oct. 21, 1864. Mustered out July 13, 1865.

Bliven, Benjamin C. Residence, Newport. 23. S. Carpenter. Enlisted Aug. 13, 1862. WIA, July 30, 1864 at the Crater, Petersburg, VA. Trans. to Co. B, 7th R.I. Vols. Oct. 21, 1864. Absent sick at Portsmouth Grove, RI, Mar. 1865, and so borne until mustered out June 16, 1865. Died Feb. 29, 1892. Interred at Oak Grove Cemetery, Fall River, MA.

Bliven, Christopher. Residence, Newport. 18. S. Laborer. Enlisted Sept. 11, 1861. WIA July 30, 1864 at the Crater, Petersburg, VA. Discharged for disability Jan. 23, 1865 at New York, NY. Died June 9, 1919. Interred at Arlington National Cemetery, Section 17, Grave 19553.

Brown, George H. Residence, Scituate. 21. S. Farmer. Enlisted Sept. 23, 1861. Deserted June 25, 1862 near Beaufort, NC.

Brown, William. Residence, Providence. 19. S. Farmer. Enlisted Sept. 25, 1861. Trans. to Co. B, 7th R.I. Vols. Oct. 21, 1864. Mustered out July 13, 1865.

Burbank, James H. Residence, Providence. 23. S. Seaman. Enlisted Sept. 25, 1861. Promoted to Sgt. Oct. 23, 1862.

Burrill, Leroy. Residence, Norwich, CT. 21. S. Shoemaker. Enlisted Sept. 25, 1861. Promoted to Corp.

Case, John R. Residence, Smithfield. 19. S. Boatman. Enlisted Sept. 23, 1861. Mustered out Oct. 15, 1864. Died Nov. 15, 1897. Interred at Ancient Little Neck Cemetery, East Providence, RI.

Cassidy, Patrick. Residence, Providence. 45. S. Agent. Enlisted Nov. 18, 1862. Mustered out Oct. 15, 1864. Died July 2, 1889. Interred at St. Mary's Cemetery, Newport, RI.

Chaill, Watt. Residence, Providence. 23. S. Laborer. Enlisted Sept. 17, 1861. Drowned Aug. 1, 1862 in the Potomac River.

Chase, Joseph. Residence, Warwick. 24. M. Seaman. Enlisted Sept. 23, 1861. Mustered out Oct. 15, 1864. Died 1867. Interred at Charles Chase Lot, North Kingstown Cemetery 16, North Kingstown, RI.

Chase, Vincent. Residence, Warwick. 28. M. Seaman. Enlisted Sept. 23, 1861. Mustered out Oct. 15, 1864.

Coggeshall, Thomas J. Residence, Warwick. 20. S. Boatman. Enlisted Sept. 23, 1861. Promoted to Corp.

Cook, Constant C. Residence, Warwick. 16. M. Baker. Enlisted July 30, 1862. Deserted in the face of the enemy Sept. 17, 1862 at Antietam, MD.

Daggett, Elisha. Residence, Burrillville. 26. S. Merchant. Enlisted Sept. 9, 1861. Discharged for disability Dec. 10, 1862 at Alexandria, VA. Interred at Capt. James Reynolds Lot, Glocester Cemetery 3, Glocester, RI.

Damon, George H. Residence, Gardiner, MA. 29. S. Jeweler. Enlisted Sept. 25, 1861. Mustered out Oct. 15, 1864. Interred at North Burial Ground, Providence, RI.

Dow, Cicero M. Residence, Bradford, ME. 18. S. Butcher. Enlisted Sept. 25, 1861. Deserted in the face of the enemy Sept. 17, 1862 at Antietam, MD. Later served in Co. B, 81st Pennsylvania Vols. under alias Henry Steele. Died Jan. 1, 1899. Interred at Walnut Hill Cemetery, Pawtucket, RI.

Driscoll, John A. Residence, Taunton, MA. 24. S. Shoemaker. Enlisted Aug. 1, 1862. Trans. to Co. B, 7th R.I. Vols. Oct. 21,

1864. Mustered out July 13, 1865. Died 1914. Interred at Hope Cemetery, Kennebunk, ME.

Dunbar, John A. Residence, Bristol. 46. S. Farmer. Enlisted Sept. 23, 1861. Mustered out Oct. 15, 1864. Died April 14, 1892. Interred at North Burial Ground, Bristol, RI.

Easterbrooks, William H. Residence, Bristol. 19. S. Farmer. Enlisted Sept. 23, 1861. CIA July 30, 1864 at the Crater, Petersburg, VA. Trans. to Co. B, 7th R.I. Vols. Oct. 21, 1864. Mustered out July 13, 1865. Died 1925. Interred at North Burial Ground, Bristol, RI.

Eckles, Edward. Residence, Newport. 38. M. Laborer. Enlisted Sept. 11, 1861. Trans. to Co. B, 7th R.I. Vols. Oct. 21, 1864. Mustered out July 13, 1865. Interred at Hampton National Cemetery, Hampton, VA. Section FII, Grave 6067.

Finnan, John. Residence, Providence. 37. M. Laborer. Enlisted Sept. 16, 1861. Discharged for disability Nov. 21, 1862 at Baltimore, MD.

Gardner, Warren D. Residence, East Greenwich. 16. S. Clerk. Enlisted Sept. 17, 1861. Discharge for disability Sept. 25, 1862 at Fort Monroe, VA. Died Nov. 28, 1923. Interred at First Presbyterian Church Cemetery, Succasunna, NJ.

Geary, Patrick. Residence, Newport. 23. S. Laborer. Enlisted Sept. 11, 1861. Mustered out Oct. 15, 1864.

Gifford, Henry C. Residence, Bristol. 26. S. Carder. Enlisted Sept. 25, 1861. Promoted to Corp. Dec. 12, 1861.

Gladding, Henry F. Residence, Bristol. 19. S. Farmer. Enlisted Sept. 25, 1861. Promoted to Corp.

Griffith, Joseph H. Residence, Providence. 18. S. Farmer. Enlisted Oct. 7, 1861. WIA, shot in left thigh May 3, 1863 near Suffolk, VA. Trans. to Co. B, 7th R.I. Vols. Oct. 21, 1864. Mustered out

July 13, 1865. Died Feb. 5, 1888. Interred at North Burial Ground, Providence, RI.

Gorton, Charles A. Residence, Warwick. 38. M. Boatman. Enlisted Sept. 23, 1861. Promoted to Corp.

Hayes, John. Residence, Burrillville. 33. S. Laborer. Enlisted Sept. 17, 1861. Trans. to Co. B, 7th R.I. Vols. Oct. 21, 1864. Mustered out July 13, 1865. Interred at St. Mary's Cemetery, West Warwick, RI.

Heath, Charles C. Residence, Newport. 31. M. Laborer. Enlisted Aug. 12, 1861. Trans. to the U.S. Navy June 1, 1864.

Hines, Francis K. Residence, Providence. 32. M. Silversmith. Enlisted Sept. 23, 1861. Mustered out Oct. 15, 1864.

Holden, Henry J. Residence, Providence. 38. M. Laborer. Enlisted Sept. 18, 1861. Discharged for disability Jan. 2, 1863 at Providence, RI. Died Aug. 6, 1882. Interred at Holden-Bicknell-Taylor Lot, Warwick Cemetery 99, Warwick, RI.

Horton, Jerome B. Residence, Burrillville. 23. M. Laborer. Enlisted Aug. 7, 1861. Died of typhoid April 29, 1862 at New Bern, NC.

Howard, George. Residence, Rochester, MA. 18. S. Farmer. Enlisted Sept. 25, 1861. Trans. to Co. B, 7th R.I. Vols. Oct. 21, 1864. Mustered out July 13, 1865.

Howard, Michael. Residence, Newport. 34. S. Laborer. Enlisted Sept. 16, 1861. Trans. to Co. B, 7th R.I. Vols. Oct. 21, 1864. Mustered out July 13, 1865.

Hudson, George A. Residence, Newport. 20. S. Farmer. Enlisted Sept. 11, 1861. Discharged for disability Mar. 20, 1863 at Providence, RI. Died January 21, 1907. Interred at Dayton National Cemetery, Dayton, OH. Section P, Row 19, Grave 27.

Kelley, James. Residence, Cranston. 23. S. Laborer. Enlisted Sept. 25, 1861. Mustered out Oct. 15, 1864.

Kiely, Michael. Residence, Newport. 20. M. Farmer. Enlisted Aug. 10, 1861. Mustered out Oct. 15, 1864.

Knight, William A. Residence, Cranston. 24. S. Laborer. Enlisted Sept. 25, 1861. WIA, left leg amputated, Sept. 17, 1862 at Antietam, MD. Discharged for disability Dec. 30, 1862 at Frederick, MD. Died Aug. 11, 1878. Interred at Swan Point Cemetery, Providence, RI.

Ingalls, Horace E. Residence, New York, NY. 20. S. Clerk. Enlisted Sept. 9, 1861. Trans. to Regular Army Nov. 28, 1862.

Livesey, Theodore. Residence, Providence. 17. S. Painter. Enlisted Sept. 23, 1861. KIA Sept. 17, 1862 at Antietam, MD. Interred at Grace Church Cemetery, Providence, RI.

Lord, Charles F. Residence, York, ME. 24. M. Machinist. Enlisted Oct. 1, 1861. Trans. to Co. B, 7th R.I. Vols. Oct. 21, 1864. Mustered out July 13, 1865. Died 1913. Interred at North Burial Ground, Providence, RI.

McCann, Francis. Residence, Charlestown, MA. 24. S. Marble cutter. Enlisted Sept. 4, 1861. Trans. to VRC Mar. 18, 1864.
McLaughlin, Thomas. Residence, Providence. 30. M. Laborer. Enlisted Sept. 17, 1861. Mustered out Oct. 15, 1864.

McKenna, John. Residence, Providence. 30. M. Laborer. Enlisted Sept. 17, 1861. Discharged for disability Feb. 28, 1863.

Manchester, George S. Residence, Providence. 19. S. Laborer. Enlisted Sept. 14, 1861. Mustered out Oct. 15, 1864.

Mason, James H. Residence, Warren. 33. M. Jeweler. Enlisted Oct. 1, 1861. WIA, shot in leg, Sept. 17, 1862 at Antietam, MD. Discharged for disability Jan. 29, 1863 at Providence, RI. Died

May 16, 1902. Interred at North Burial Ground, Bristol, RI.
Interred at North Burial Ground, Providence, RI.

Masterson, Patrick. Residence, Newport. 21. S. Laborer. Enlisted Sept. 11, 1861. Trans. to Co. B, 7th R.I. Vols. Oct. 21, 1864. Mustered out July 13, 1865.

Moore, Andrew S. Residence, Camden, ME. 36. M. Laborer. Enlisted Sept. 11, 1861. Died of tuberculosis Nov. 29, 1863 at Portsmouth, RI.

Myers, Abraham. Residence, Stockbridge, MA. 19. S. Weaver. Enlisted Sept. 19, 1861. Trans. to Co. B, 7th R.I. Vols. Oct. 21, 1864. Mustered out July 13, 1865. Died 1915. Interred at North Burial Ground, Bristol, RI.

Pierce, Leonard. Residence, Swansea, MA. 43. M. Mason. Enlisted Sept. 9, 1861. Discharged for disability Sept. 21, 1863 at Portsmouth, RI. Died July 27, 1884. Interred at Togus National Cemetery, Augusta, ME. Grave 416.

Riley, James. Residence, Newport. 23. S. Farmer. Enlisted Sept. 11, 1862. Trans. to Co. B, 7th R.I. Vols. Oct. 21, 1864. Mustered out July 13, 1865. Died May 8, 1911. Interred at Waverly Cemetery, Waverly, KS.

Scott, Russell I. Residence, Dedham, MA. 17. S. Clerk. Enlisted Sept. 25, 1861. Discharged for disability Dec. 7, 1862. Interred at Grace Church Cemetery, Providence, RI.

Shay, Jeremiah. Residence, Newport. 35. M. Laborer. Enlisted Sept. 11, 1861. Trans. to Co. B, 7th R.I. Vols. Oct. 21, 1864. Mustered out July 13, 1865.

Shumway, Charles E. Residence, Burrillville. 19. S. Stone cutter. Enlisted Sept. 9, 1861. Mustered out Oct. 15, 1864. Promoted to Corp. July 30, 1864.

Shippee, William J. Residence, Bristol. 29. S. Farmer. Enlisted Sept. 24, 1861. Trans. to Co. B, 7th R.I. Vols. Oct. 21, 1864. Mustered out July 13, 1865. Died 1877. Interred at North Burial Ground, Bristol, RI.

Slocum, Charles F. Residence, Warwick. 21. S. Clerk. Enlisted Sept. 23, 1861. Trans. to Co. B, 7th R.I. Vols. Oct. 21, 1864. Died Sept. 23, 1879. Interred at Lakewood Burial Ground, Warwick, RI.

Smith, David C. Residence, Middletown. 21. S. Farmer. Enlisted July 31, 1862. Trans. to Co. B, 7th R.I. Vols. Oct. 21, 1864. Mustered out July 13, 1865. Died 1925. Interred at Middletown Cemetery, Middletown, RI.

Spooner, Horatio. Residence, Plymouth, MA. 36. M. Machinist. Enlisted Sept. 17, 1861. Mustered out Oct. 15, 1864.

Sullivan, Daniel. Residence, Newport. 21. S. Gardiner. Enlisted Sept. 11, 1861. Trans. to Co. B, 7th R.I. Vols. Oct. 21, 1864. Mustered out July 13, 1865.

Sweet, Ferdinand. Residence, North Providence. 21. S. Teamster. Enlisted Sept. 23, 1861. Promoted to Corp. Dec. 12, 1861.

Tabor, John N. Residence, Coventry. 26. S. Pharmacist. Enlisted Aug. 30, 1862. Discharged for disability Mar. 26, 1863 at Washington, DC. Interred at Oakland Cemetery, Cranston, RI.

Thurber, John H. Residence, Newport. 18. S. Miller. Enlisted Sept. 23, 1861. Trans. to the Regular Army Jan. 15, 1863.

Tompkins, Daniel. Residence, Providence. 18. S. Farmer. Enlisted Sept. 12, 1861. Discharged for disability June 11, 1863. Died of disease contracted in the service Sept. 10, 1863. Interred at Oak Grove Cemetery, Fall River, MA.

Vizard, James. Residence, Newport. 38. M. Laborer. Enlisted Sept. 12, 1861. Trans. to VRC Sept. 1, 1863.

Waterman, George F. Residence, Johnston. 25. S. Pharmacist. Enlisted Sept. 23, 1861. Promoted to 2nd Lt. Co. C, Jan. 13, 1863.

Weaver, Benoni. Residence, Middletown. 42. M. Farmer. Enlisted July 30, 1862. KIA Sept. 17, 1862 at Antietam, MD. Interred at Antietam National Cemetery, Sharpsburg, MD. Rhode Island Section, Grave 2825. Cenotaph at Island Cemetery, Newport, RI.

Weeden, William H. Residence, Johnston. 19. S. Farmer. Enlisted Sept. 25, 1861. Mustered out Oct. 15, 1864. Died July 3, 1900. Interred at Pocasset Cemetery, Cranston, RI.

Weeks, William A. Residence, Hopkinton. 22. S. Farmer. Enlisted Sept. 27, 1861. CIA Sept. 17, 1862 at Antietam, MD. Mustered out Oct. 15, 1864. Died 1925. Interred at Robbins Cemetery, Voluntown, CT.

Wiley, George N. Residence, Coventry. 21. S. Engineer. Enlisted Aug. 8, 1862. Deserted in the face of the enemy Sept. 17, 1862 at Antietam, MD. Died 1926. Interred at North Burial Ground, Providence, RI.

Wiley, William A. Residence, Coventry. 53. S. Farmer. Enlisted Aug. 11, 1862. Mustered out Oct. 15, 1864. Died Oct. 29, 1888. Interred at Grace Church Cemetery, Providence, RI.

Wilmarth, Joseph. Residence, Bristol. 21. S. Seaman. Enlisted Oct. 4, 1861. Mustered out Oct. 15, 1864. Died 1897. Interred at Oak Hill Cemetery, Woonsocket, RI.

ENLISTSMENTS BY TOWN

Town	Number of men
Barrington	0
Bristol	10
Burrillville	41
Charlestown	11
Coventry	45
Cranston	12
Cumberland	30
East Greenwich	12
East Providence	0
Exeter	8
Foster	1
Glocester	19
Hopkinton	15
Jamestown	1
Johnston	18
Little Compton	0
Middletown	7
New Shoreham	2
Newport	120
North Kingstown	63
North Providence	3
Pawtucket	16
Portsmouth	2
Providence	274
Richmond	7
Scituate	15

Smithfield	59
South Kingstown	12
Tiverton	16
Warren	4
Warwick	57
West Greenwich	0
Westerly	15
Woonsocket	47
Connecticut	9
Massachusetts	51
Maine	5
New Hampshire	3
Vermont	1
New York	8
Regimental Total	1019

REGIMENTAL STATISTICS

Field and Staff

Died of Disease	0
Accidental Death	0
Died of Disease after mustered out	2
Mustered out of service	11
Transferred to 7th R.I. Vols.	2
Discharged for Disability	1
Transferred to Veterans Reserve Corps	0
Resigned	7
Dismissed from the service	0
Promoted to other unit	1
Trans. to U.S. Army	0
Trans. to U.S. Navy	0
Deserted	0

Combat Casualties

Battle	Killed/Mortally	Wounded	Captured	Total
Roanoke	0	0	0	0
New Bern	0	2	0	2
Fort Macon	0	0	0	0
South Mountain	0	0	0	0
Antietam	0	1	0	1
Fredericksburg	1	0	0	1
Suffolk	0	0	0	0
Petersburg (trenches)	0	0	0	0
Petersburg (Crater)	0	0	1	1
Weldon Railroad	0	0	0	0
Hatcher's Run	0	0	0	0

Poplar Spring Church	0	0	0	0
Total	1	3	1	5

Regimental Band

Died of Disease	0
Accidental Death	0
Died of Disease after mustered out	0
Mustered out of service	19
Transferred to 7th R.I. Vols.	0
Discharged for Disability	0
Transferred to Veterans Reserve Corps	0
Resigned	0
Dismissed from the service	0
Promoted to other unit	0
Trans. to U.S. Army	0
Trans. to U.S. Navy	0
Deserted	0

Combat Casualties

Battle	Killed/Mortally	Wounded	Captured	Total
Roanoke	0	0	0	0
New Bern	0	0	0	0
Fort Macon	0	0	0	0
South Mountain	0	0	0	0
Antietam	0	1	0	0
Fredericksburg	0	0	0	0
Suffolk	0	0	0	0
Petersburg (trenches)	0	0	0	0
Petersburg (Crater)	0	0	0	0
Weldon Railroad	0	0	0	0
Hatcher's Run	0	0	0	0
Poplar Spring Church	0	0	0	0

| Total | 0 | 1 | 0 | 1 |

Company A

Died of Disease	6
Accidental Death	2
Died of Disease after mustered out	1
Mustered out of service	28
Transferred to 7th R.I. Vols.	23
Discharged for Disability	19
Transferred to Veterans Reserve Corps	4
Resigned	2
Dismissed from the service	1
Promoted to other unit	1
Trans. to U.S. Army	2
Trans. to U.S. Navy	0
Deserted	3

Combat Casualties

Battle	Killed/Mortally	Wounded	Captured	Total
Roanoke	1	0	0	1
New Bern	1	0	0	1
Fort Macon	0	0	0	0
South Mountain	0	0	0	0
Antietam	1	10	0	11
Fredericksburg	0	0	0	0
Suffolk	1	1	0	2
Petersburg (trenches)	0	0	0	0
Petersburg (Crater)	5	7	3	15
Weldon Railroad	0	0	0	0
Hatcher's Run	0	0	0	0
Poplar Spring Church	0	0	0	0
Total	9	18	3	30

Company B

Died of Disease	8
Accidental Death	0
Died of Disease after mustered out	1
Mustered out of service	33
Transferred to 7th R.I. Vols.	17
Discharged for Disability	21
Transferred to Veterans Reserve Corps	3
Resigned	2
Dismissed from the service	1
Promoted to other unit	0
Trans. to U.S. Army	0
Trans. to U.S. Navy	1
Deserted	5

Combat Casualties

Battle	Killed/Mortally	Wounded	Captured	Total
Roanoke	0	1	0	1
New Bern	2	3	0	5
Fort Macon	0	0	0	0
South Mountain	0	0	0	0
Antietam	11	4	0	15
Fredericksburg	0	0	0	0
Suffolk	0	3	0	3
Petersburg (trenches)	1	2	0	3
Petersburg (Crater)	2	0	1	3
Weldon Railroad	0	0	0	0
Hatcher's Run	0	0	0	0
Poplar Spring Church	0	0	0	0
Total	16	13	1	30

Company C

Died of Disease	8
Accidental Death	0
Died of Disease after mustered out	1
Mustered out of service	16
Transferred to 7th R.I. Vols.	31
Discharged for Disability	19
Transferred to Veterans Reserve Corps	6
Resigned	3
Dismissed from the service	0
Promoted to other unit	1
Trans. to U.S. Army	1
Trans. to U.S. Navy	2
Deserted	18

Combat Casualties

Battle	Killed/Mortally	Wounded	Captured	Total
Roanoke	0	0	0	0
New Bern	3	2	0	5
Fort Macon	0	0	0	0
South Mountain	0	0	0	0
Antietam	2	5	0	7
Fredericksburg	0	1	0	1
Suffolk	0	1	0	1
Petersburg (trenches)	2	0	0	2
Petersburg (Crater)	3	6	2	11
Weldon Railroad	0	0	0	0
Hatcher's Run	0	0	0	0
Poplar Spring Church	0	0	0	0

| Total | 10 | 15 | 2 | 27 |

Company D

Died of Disease	5
Accidental Death	1
Died of Disease after mustered out	1
Mustered out of service	30
Transferred to 7th R.I. Vols.	16
Discharged for Disability	20
Transferred to Veterans Reserve Corps	1
Resigned	3
Dismissed from the service	0
Promoted to other unit	0
Trans. to U.S. Army	1
Trans. to U.S. Navy	0
Deserted	5

Combat Casualties

Battle	Killed/Mortally	Wounded	Captured	Total
Roanoke	0	0	0	0
New Bern	4	2	0	6
Fort Macon	0	0	0	0
South Mountain	0	0	0	0
Antietam	7	5	0	12
Fredericksburg	0	1	0	1
Suffolk	0	0	0	0
Petersburg (trenches)	0	0	0	0
Petersburg (Crater)	1	4	3	8
Weldon Railroad	0	0	0	0
Hatcher's Run	1	0	0	1
Poplar Spring Church	0	0	0	0
Total	13	12	3	28

Company E

Died of Disease	2
Accidental Death	0
Died of Disease after mustered out	0
Mustered out of service	23
Transferred to 7th R.I. Vols.	33
Discharged for Disability	16
Transferred to Veterans Reserve Corps	0
Resigned	1
Dismissed from the service	1
Promoted to other unit	0
Trans. to U.S. Army	1
Trans. to U.S. Navy	0
Deserted	9

Combat Casualties

Battle	Killed/Mortally	Wounded	Captured	Total
Roanoke	0	0	0	0
New Bern	1	2	0	3
Fort Macon	0	0	0	0
South Mountain	0	1	0	1
Antietam	2	10	0	12
Fredericksburg	0	1	0	1
Suffolk	0	0	0	0
Petersburg (trenches)	1	1	0	2
Petersburg (Crater)	1	8	2	11
Weldon Railroad	0	0	0	0
Hatcher's Run	0	0	0	0
Poplar Spring Church	0	0	0	0
Total	5	23	2	30

Company F

Died of Disease	7
Accidental Death	0
Died of Disease after mustered out	2
Mustered out of service	18
Transferred to 7th R.I. Vols.	30
Discharged for Disability	20
Transferred to Veterans Reserve Corps	4
Resigned	0
Dismissed from the service	1
Promoted to other unit	1
Trans. to U.S. Army	1
Trans. to U.S. Navy	0
Deserted	3

Combat Casualties

Battle	Killed/Mortally	Wounded	Captured	Total
Roanoke	0	0	0	0
New Bern	1	3	0	4
Fort Macon	0	0	0	0
South Mountain	0	1	0	1
Antietam	2	14	0	16
Fredericksburg	0	4	0	4
Suffolk	0	0	0	0
Petersburg (trenches)	0	0	0	0
Petersburg (Crater)	0	7	1	8
Weldon Railroad	0	0	0	0
Hatcher's Run	0	0	0	0
Poplar Spring Church	0	0	0	0
Total	3	29	1	33

Company G

Died of Disease	9
Accidental Death	1
Died of Disease after mustered out	3
Mustered out of service	33
Transferred to 7th R.I. Vols.	17
Discharged for Disability	21
Transferred to Veterans Reserve Corps	3
Resigned	5
Dismissed from the service	0
Promoted to other unit	0
Trans. to U.S. Army	0
Trans. to U.S. Navy	4
Deserted	0

Combat Casualties

Battle	Killed/Mortally	Wounded	Captured	Total
Roanoke	0	0	0	0
New Bern	0	0	0	0
Fort Macon	0	0	0	0
South Mountain	0	0	0	0
Antietam	4	8	0	12
Fredericksburg	0	2	0	2
Suffolk	0	2	0	2
Petersburg (trenches)	1	0	0	1
Petersburg (Crater)	0	4	1	5
Weldon Railroad	0	0	0	0
Hatcher's Run	0	0	0	0
Poplar Spring Church	3	0	0	3
Total	8	16	1	25

Company H

Died of Disease	10
Accidental Death	0
Died of Disease after mustered out	2
Mustered out of service	31
Transferred to 7th R.I. Vols.	19
Discharged for Disability	18
Transferred to Veterans Reserve Corps	1
Resigned	1
Dismissed from the service	1
Promoted to other unit	0
Trans. to U.S. Army	0
Trans. to U.S. Navy	0
Deserted	2

Combat Casualties

Battle	Killed/Mortally	Wounded	Captured	Total
Roanoke	0	0	0	0
New Bern	3	1	0	4
Fort Macon	0	0	0	0
South Mountain	0	0	0	0
Antietam	1	5	1	7
Fredericksburg	0	0	0	0
Suffolk	0	0	0	0
Petersburg (trenches)	0	0	0	0
Petersburg (Crater)	1	7	3	11
Weldon Railroad	0	0	0	0
Hatcher's Run	0	0	0	0
Poplar Spring Church	0	1	0	1
Total	5	14	4	23

Company I

Died of Disease	4
Accidental Death	0
Died of Disease after mustered out	0
Mustered out of service	36
Transferred to 7th R.I. Vols.	14
Discharged for Disability	24
Transferred to Veterans Reserve Corps	4
Resigned	2
Dismissed from the service	0
Promoted to other unit	1
Trans. to U.S. Army	4
Trans. to U.S. Navy	0
Deserted	0

Combat Casualties

Battle	Killed/Mortally	Wounded	Captured	Total
Roanoke	0	0	0	0
New Bern	1	1	0	2
Fort Macon	0	0	0	0
South Mountain	0	0	0	0
Antietam	6	10	1	17
Fredericksburg	0	0	0	0
Suffolk	0	0	0	0
Petersburg (trenches)	0	0	0	0
Petersburg (Crater)	0	2	3	5
Weldon Railroad	0	0	0	0
Hatcher's Run	0	0	0	0
Poplar Spring Church	0	0	0	0
Total	7	13	4	24

Company K

Died of Disease	3
Accidental Death	1
Died of Disease after mustered out	2
Mustered out of service	25
Transferred to 7th R.I. Vols.	24
Discharged for Disability	19
Transferred to Veterans Reserve Corps	2
Resigned	3
Dismissed from the service	0
Promoted to other unit	0
Trans. to U.S. Army	2
Trans. to U.S. Navy	1
Deserted	4

Combat Casualties

Battle	Killed/Mortally	Wounded	Captured	Total
Roanoke	0	0	0	0
New Bern	0	0	0	0
Fort Macon	0	0	0	0
South Mountain	0	0	0	0
Antietam	2	3	0	5
Fredericksburg	0	0	0	0
Suffolk	0	1	0	1
Petersburg (trenches)	0	0	0	0
Petersburg (Crater)	1	6	2	9
Weldon Railroad	0	0	0	0
Hatcher's Run	0	0	0	0
Poplar Spring Church	0	0	0	0
Total	3	10	2	15

REGIMENTAL TOTALS

Died of Disease	62
Accidental Death	5
Died of Disease after mustered out	15
Mustered out of service	301
Transferred to 7th R.I. Vols.	226
Discharged for Disability	199
Transferred to Veterans Reserve Corps	28
Resigned	29
Dismissed from the service	5
Promoted to other unit	5
Trans. to U.S. Army	12
Trans. to U.S. Navy	8
Deserted	56

Combat Casualties

Battle	Killed/Mortally	Wounded	Captured	Total
Roanoke	1	1	0	2
New Bern	16	16	0	32
Fort Macon	0	0	0	0
South Mountain	0	2	0	2
Antietam	38	75	3	116
Fredericksburg	1	9	0	10
Suffolk	1	8	0	9
Petersburg (trenches)	5	3	0	8
Petersburg (Crater)	14	51	22	87
Weldon Railroad	0	0	0	0
Hatcher's Run	1	0	0	1
Poplar Spring Church	3	1	0	4
Total	80	166	25	271

THE RHODE ISLAND DEAD

AT NEWBERN

During the Civil War, memorial poetry became a popular medium in the North to commemorate the soldiers and sailors who died in the conflict. These poems provided family members and the communities that they came from with a lasting tribute to the sacrifices that they made to preserve the Union and free the slave. Often written by someone who knew the deceased, lines from these poems were often used to adorn the memorial to the fallen. These poems frequently told that the soldier had not died in vain, that they had fallen for a glorious cause, while also exalting those who remained at home to go and enlist to carry on their cause. They remain a powerful reminder of the sacrifice made by the Civil War generation; of 23,000 Rhode Islanders who fought in the Civil War, over 2,000 never came home.

The poem below was written by William A. Boss in honor of two soldiers from North Kingstown, Sergeant George H. Church and Private Charles Baker, both of Company H, Fourth Rhode Island Volunteers. Both men were killed at New Bern, North Carolina on March 14, 1862. The remains of both men were returned to their native town on April 16, 1862, and in one of the largest funerals ever seen in North Kingstown, both soldiers were interred at Elm Grove Cemetery. As the first Civil War battle deaths from North Kingstown, the loss of these two men touched the community. Baker was only seventeen when he died; after the war, the veterans of Wickford would name their local Grand Army of the Republic Post, C.C. Baker Post 16 in his honor.

William A. Boss is known to have written at least three poems in honor of deceased Rhode Island soldiers. Little information can be gathered about his life. This poem was published as a broadside in Wickford in 1862. In it, Boss mourns the loss of Church and Baker, while also urging Rhode Islanders to enlist in the Union cause. This poem could also be sung, as Boss intended, to the tune of "California Brother." The below is a full transcription of Boss' work, taken from the only known surviving copy at the John Hay Library at Brown University, Providence, Rhode Island. Although originally intended to honor two soldiers from North Kingstown, it is a fitting tribute to all of the officers and men of the Fighting Fourth Rhode Island Volunteers who gave the last full measure of devotion in the War for the Preservation of the Union.

The Rhode Island Dead at Newbern,

In allusion to Sergeant George H. Church, and Private Charles Baker, of Wickford, R.I., who were killed at the battle of Newbern, N.C. in March 1862.

By Wm. A. Boss.

Tune- "California Brother"

Sweetly sleep, thou fallen heroes,
In thy long, unbroken rest;
Now no more shall cruel warfare
E'er disturb thy tranquil breast.
Thou didst gain the brightest laurels
When at Newbern though didst fall-
Hoisted there our nation's banner,
On the vile Secesh's soil.

Thou hast won a glorious victory,
And has fallen in the scene;
But the lips of unborn millions
Yet shall bless thy honored names,
Yet shall calls thy names with rapture,
And shall tell thy noble deeds:
That ye sought to crush rebellion
On the bloody battle field.

For thy fall thy friends are mourning,
And their hearts are bowed in woe,
For they shall no more forever
Gaze upon thy noble brow.
Yet they have a source of comfort
When they think upon the fate,
That ye died till death contending
For the Union of the States.

Mourn ye not, friends in sadness,
For my loved ones true and bold;
They have reached a better country,
Where no foes they'll e'er behold-
Where they'll hear no cry of battle
On that peaceful happy shore,
But with peace and joy meandering,
They will dwell forevermore.

We have borne them to Rhode Island,
In her soil to find a tomb,
Here, oh here, we have interred them,
By their kindred, friends, and home.
Here we'd set the waving willow,
By their loved and honored graves;
Here we'd drop the tear if sorrow
For the valiant and the brave.

Honored be the youthful martyrs
To their country's sacrifice cause,
Bravely fought they for the Union
To sustain her noble laws.
May their mem'ries be embalmed
In the hearts of patriots true;
May our banners float triumphant
O'er our prostrate rebel foe.

Rouse! Rhode Island's sons get ready!
Hear our country's call for aid,

Hasten to the plains of battle,
And avenge the noble dead.
Oh, sustain thy nation's banner,
Keep it free from treasons stain,
Till we hear the welcome tidings-
"Peace unto our land again."

When the echoing voice of Freedom
Shall roll o'er Columbia's plain.
And from home, and vale, and mountain,
Shall be heard the joyful strain.
Then we'll bless the God of Nations
For His love, and power, and might,
That he kept us through the darkness
Of rebellion's dismal night.

FURTHER READING

Allen, George H. *Forty-Six Months with the Fourth R.I. Volunteers, in the War of 1861 to 1865 Comprising a History of Its Marches, Battles, and Camp Life. Compiled from Journals Kept While on Duty in the Field and Camp, by Corp. Geo. H. Allen.* Providence: J.A. & R.A. Reid, 1887.

Originally published as his memoirs, this book was later adopted by the Fourth Rhode Island veterans as their official regimental history. A corporal from Providence, Allen kept a meticulous journal during the war. This volume provides one of the best accounts of the Battle of New Bern, as well as the Fourth's actions at Antietam and the Crater at Petersburg. Highly readable, Allen wrote clearly and with a sense of preserving the deeds of his regiment for posterity. The book also provides details regarding the bitter feud between the Fourth and Seventh Rhode Island Regiments.

Bartlett, John Russell. *Memoirs of Rhode Island Officers: Who were Engaged in the Service of their Country During the Great Rebellion of the South.* Providence: Sydney S. Rider, 1867.

A great resource that provides valuable information on the officer corps of the Fourth Rhode Island.

Cady, John Hutchins. *Rhode Island Boundaries, 1636-1936.* Providence: Rhode Island Tercentenary Commission, 1936.

Rhode Island's boundaries have shifted tremendously since the Fourth Rhode Island was recruited in 1861. This book is especially helpful in understanding what towns the men enlisted from.

Chartrand, Rene. "O Canada!: Canada's National Anthem: Composed by Calixa Lavallee, 4th Rhode Island Regiment, 1861-1862." *Military Collector and Historian* Vol. 53, No. 3 (Fall 2001), 110.

A brief but interesting article regarding the unique uniform worn by the band of the Fourth Rhode Island during their service; the band was mustered out shortly after Antietam.

Civil War Letters of Hugh McInnes. Parsons, WV: McClain Publishing, 1981.

McInnes was from Richmond and served as a sergeant in Company A of the Fourth Rhode Island; he lost an arm at the Battle of the Crater, July 30, 1864. These are above average soldier's letters with McInnes frequently writing home about life in the South. Of particular importance are letters written about the Burnside Expedition, Antietam, and his interactions with other Rhode Island soldiers. This book is exceptionally rare.

Cummings, S.S. *Life and Work of Rev. S.S. Cummings, Pastor, Chaplain, Delegate of Christian Commission, Missionary Agent of N.E. Home for Little Wanderers Twenty-Nine Years.* Sommerville, MA: NP, 1898.

Cummings served during the war as the chaplain of the Fourth Rhode Island. His letters home to his family is included in the book and provides interesting details regarding the service of a minister during the war.

Dyer, Elisha, *Annual Report of the Adjutant General of Rhode Island and Providence Plantations, for the Year 1865.* Providence: E.L. Freeman & Son, 1893.

More often cited as the *Revised Register of Rhode Island Volunteers*. Volume One contains the infantry enlistments from Rhode Island and Volume Two contains the men who joined the artillery, cavalry, and Regular Army, as well as the Navy and Marine Corps. This book is a great reference and was the building block to building the roster in this book, however it does contain many errors.

Grandchamp, Robert. "Martyrs to the Cause of Liberty: Hopkinton Boys of the Fighting Fourth." *Rhode Island Roots* Vol. 40, No. 3 (September 2014), 135-143.

An interesting transcription and accompanying text of a long letter printed in the *Narragansett Weekly* of Westerly written by a soldier from Hopkinton who served in the Fourth. In the fall of 1861, nine students from the local Hopkinton Academy enlisted in the Fourth, four of whom would die in the Civil War. This article provides information on these men and their experiences at New Bern, Antietam, and in camp.

Hopkins, William P. *The Seventh Rhode Island Volunteers in the Civil War:1862-1865.* Providence: Snow & Farnum, 1903.

The official history of the Seventh Rhode Island was written by a drummer in Company D. It is lavishly illustrated with hundreds of images, as well as full of biographical details of members of the regiment. Written in a diary format, it has been cited as among the finest of post-war regimental histories. Provides information on the Fourth, after its consolidation with the Seventh.

Nelson, Sebastian. "The Greene Brothers Civil War." *Military Images* Vol. 29, No. 3 (November/December 2007), 28-33.

A very interesting photograph of the five Greene brothers who served in the Civil War. Daniel H. Greene served in the Fourth Rhode Island, while Willard served in the Twelfth Rhode Island Volunteers. Edward W. Greene was in the Twenty-Ninth Massachusetts, Jerome B. Greene in Battery I, First New York Artillery, and Henry A. Greene in the First California Infantry. Includes detailed analysis of the photograph and brief biographies of each brother.

Proceedings at the Dedication of the Soldiers' and Sailors' Monument, in Providence: To Which Is Appended a List of the Deceased Soldiers and Sailors Whose Names Are Sculptured Upon the Monument. Providence: A.C. Greene, 1871.

The official program for the 1871 dedication of Rhode Island's monument to her Civil War dead in Providence. The book contains a roster of the deceased Rhode Island soldiers and these names were used to cross-reference against the roster in this book.

Pullen, Drew. *Portrait of the Past: The Civil War on Roanoke Island North Carolina: A Pictorial Tour.* Mt. Holly, NJ: Aerial Perspective, 2002.

This is pictorial history of Roanoke Island, North Carolina, one of the early targets of the Burnside Expedition in February-March 1862. Filled with many modern photographs of the sites, as well as historical images and maps. Pullen quotes many letters in this volume from Captain William Chace of the Fourth Rhode Island who was later wounded at New Bern. The originals of the Chace letters are at the Rhode Island Historical Society.

Report of the Commissioner of the Fourth Regiment Rhode Island Volunteers to His Excellency Royal C. Taft, Governor of Rhode Island. Providence: E.L. Freeman & Son, 1889.

Further information regarding the Fourth Rhode Island clothing scandal.

Report of His Excellency George Peabody Wetmore, Governor, Relative to the Clothing Account of Fourth Regiment Rhode Island Volunteers, Etc. Providence: E.L. Freeman & Son, 1886.

When the Fourth Rhode Island was mustered in to the service in the fall of 1861, the men were charged $36.50 for their initial suit of military clothes; these should have been given free to the enlisted men. This is the first in a series of interesting pamphlets published by the state in which the veterans spent nearly thirty years trying to get their money back.

Shearman, Sumner U. *Battle of the Crater; and Experiences of Prison Life.* Providence: The Society, 1898.

Captain Shearman commanded a company in the Fourth Rhode Island and was captured at the Crater on July 30, 1864. In this important sketch, Shearman provides excellent detail into the role of the Fourth Rhode Island in the battle, as well as his subsequent imprisonment in Richmond.

Special Report of the Adjutant General in relation to the Reimbursement of the Members of the Late Fourth Rhode Island Volunteers, January 1st, 1892. Providence: E.L. Freeman & Son, 1892.

This pamphlet chronicles the resolution of the Fourth Rhode Island clothing scandal. In 1892, each veteran or their surviving family members was paid nearly one hundred dollars to settle the issue. This pamphlet provides a listing of surviving veterans of the Fourth.

Spooner, Henry Joshua. *The Maryland Campaign with the Fourth Rhode Island.* Providence: The Society, 1903.

A Brown University graduate, Spooner served as a lieutenant in the Fourth Rhode Island and later served five terms in the United States House of Representatives. The Maryland Campaign was the first for Spooner. He writes a superb narrative about being a new officer in a combat unit in the later summer of 1862. Spooner's work is a detailed and gripping account of the terrible ordeal endured by the Fourth Rhode Island in Otto's Cornfield at Antietam. Forming the extreme left flank of the Union Army, the Fourth sustained nearly fifty percent casualties when they were ambushed in the cornfield. This is one of the better publications of the Soldiers and Sailors Historical Society.

Stone, Edwin W. *Rhode Island in the Rebellion.* Providence: George H. Whitney, 1865.

Written while the Civil War was still being fought, this book is perhaps the best single volume source for general information about Rhode Island's role in the Civil War.

Thompson, Brian C. *Anthems and Minstrel Shows: The Life and Times of Calixa Lavallée, 1842-1891.* Montreal: McGill-Queen's University Press, 2015.

Calixa Lavallee is perhaps the most famous man to serve in a Rhode Island regiment during the war. A Quebecois migrant, he performed in a well-received traveling show in the United States before the war. He enlisted in the band of the Fourth Rhode Island, served in the Burnside Expedition, and was wounded at Antietam; he was discharged shortly after. In 1880, Lavallee wrote the lyrics to "O, Canada," which later became the Canadian national anthem. This book is a full biography of Lavallee.

VanDenBossche, Kris. "War and Other Reminiscences." *Rhode Island History* Vol. 47, No. 4 (November 1989), 109-147.

One of the most detailed published memoirs written by a Rhode Island soldier, this is the transcribed and annotated memoirs of Hopkinton resident Sergeant George Bradford Carpenter of Company D of the Fourth Rhode Island; the original of these memoirs is housed at the Westerly Public Library. Carpenter wrote a detailed missive of his service with excellent details about the Burnside Expedition and the Battle of the Crater where he lost his arm.

ACKNOWLEDGEMENTS

At the Rhode Island State Archives, Ken Carlson was instrumental in finding many of the smaller government publications. As always, Kris VanDenBossche pointed me in the path of some of the smaller sources and provided access to his wonderful collection.

In Providence, General Richard Valente provided access to the Benefit Street Arsenal and its vast resources while I was working on the book *Rhody Redlegs*. The staffs at the Rhode Island Historical Society, Providence City Hall Archives, Brown University, and the Providence Public Library were equally helpful.

To the clerks of every city and town hall I visited in Rhode Island, thank you. I am especially indebted to the staff at the halls in Scituate, Glocester, Coventry, Foster, Hopkinton, and Pawtucket.

Captain Phil DiMaria of Battery B has been a mentor, friend, and guide for nearly twenty years as I navigated and researched the role of Rhode Island in the Civil War era. Without Phil's assistance and guidance, none of this work would have been possible.

Mike Lannigan, Leo Kennedy, Steve Hackett, Caleb Horton, and Tom Rousseau of the Zenas R. Bliss Camp # 12 of the Sons of Union Veterans of the Civil War all provided assistance and companionship while tracking down the final resting places of these veterans.

Nina Wright and the staff at the Westerly Public Library always provided access and many photocopies when I visited that wonderful institution, as did Matt Reardon of the New England Civil War Museum in Rockville, Connecticut.

At the Varnum Continentals, Patrick Donovan provided access to the collections and listened to my many stories.

Midge Frazel helped in ways too important to list.

Cherry Fletcher Bamberg of the Rhode Island Genealogical Society is to be commended to guiding my research and writing over the years as I wrote many articles for Rhode Island Roots. I am also indebted to Rachel Peirce and the other Fourth Rhode Island descendants I have met through the Rhode Island Genealogical Society for providing me information on their ancestors.

Master Sergeant Jim Loffler, the historical section chief of the Rhode Island National Guard was helpful in tracking down the burial locations of some veterans.

I particularly want to thank the staffs at, Arlington National Cemetery, Fredericksburg and Spotsylvania National Military Park, Richmond National Battlefield, and Petersburg National Battlefield for providing burial information on Fourth Rhode Island veterans buried there.

Furthermore, I wish to thank the many property owners whose backyards I have visited to locate cemeteries on private property. As well as the Providence Water Supply Board for allowing me to visit the final resting place of my Knight ancestors.

John Sterling and his colleagues who have produced the famed "Rhode Island Cemetery Books," provided an invaluable resource.

John Fenton, U.S. Army veteran, descendant of a Fourth Rhode Island soldier, and fellow collector helped in many ways, including assisting to locate several grave locations I had missed.

Although many years have passed, the interlibrary loan staff and Marlene Lopes at Rhode Island College Special Collections will always be remembered for their assistance in finding long lost books and articles while I was a student there from 2004-2010.

Many of these sources were found in various repositories throughout Rhode Island and although I may not have remembered names, I do wish to thank these institutions that assisted in this work: Langworthy Public Library, East Providence Historical Society, Foster Preservation Society, Scituate Preservation Society, Newport Historical Society, Redwood Library, Burrillville Historical and Preservation Society, Pettaquamscutt Historical Society, Glocester Heritage Society, Bristol Historical Society, North Kingstown Public Library, East Greenwich Public Library, Westerly Armory Foundation, and the South County Museum.

Lastly, I must thank my dear wife Elizabeth. She has the patience of a saint and gladly lives with the Civil War every day.

ABOUT THE AUTHOR

Robert Grandchamp first became interested in Rhode Island's role in the Civil War in 2001, after learning from his grandmother that his third great uncle, Alfred Sheldon Knight had served in the Seventh Rhode Island Volunteers as a private in Company C, and died of pneumonia serving in the Civil War. Trips to battlefields, libraries, and archives fueled his interest and he soon began to collect material for a regimental history of the Seventh Rhode Island that was published in 2008 as *The Seventh Rhode Island Infantry in the Civil War*. Among his other works are *"We Lost Many Brave Men," In Te Domine Speramus, Rhody Redlegs, The Boys of Adams' Battery G, Colonel Edward E. Cross, Rhode Island and the Civil War: Voices from the Ocean State,* and *A Connecticut Yankee at War: The Life and Letters of George Lee Gaskell*. In total, he has authored fourteen books on military history. Robert earned his M.A. in American history from Rhode Island College, in addition to his B.A. in anthropology and American history from Rhode Island College as well. He is a former National Park Ranger with service at Shenandoah and Harpers Ferry battlefield. He has also worked at the Paine House Museum in Coventry, and at the Wilbur Kelly House at the Blackstone Valley National Corridor. For his efforts to honor the soldiers from Rhode Island, Robert has been awarded the Order of Saint Barbara from the Rhode Island National Guard, the Margaret B. Stillwell Prize from the John Russell Bartlett Society at Brown University, as well as letters of commendation from the governor of Rhode Island and mayor of Providence. Among his professional affiliations, he is a longtime member of several historical organizations, including the Rhode Island Genealogical Society. He is a Past Department Commander of the Sons of Union Veterans of the Civil War, and serves as an officer in Ethan Allen Lodge # 72 of the Free and Accepted Masons of Vermont. Robert is a senior analyst with the Federal government and resides with his wife Elizabeth and their children in Jericho Center, Vermont.

www.ingramcontent.com/pod-product-compliance
Lightning Source LLC
Chambersburg PA
CBHW062040220426
43662CB00010B/1578